THE CARD

THE CARD

WAGNER, PITTSBURG

COLLECTORS, CON MEN,

AND THE TRUE STORY OF

HISTORY'S MOST

DESIRED BASEBALL CARD

MICHAEL O'KEEFFE & TERI THOMPSON

wm WILLIAM MORROW *An Imprint of* HarperCollins*Publishers*

HarperCollins books may be purchased for educational, business, or sales promotional use. For information please write: Special Markets Department, HarperCollins Publishers, 10 East 53rd Street, New York, NY 10022.

FIRST EDITION

Designed by Susan Walsh

Library of Congress Cataloging-in-Publication Data

O'Keeffe, Michael, sports journalist.
    The card: collectors, con men, and the true story of history's most desired baseball card / Michael O'Keeffe and Teri Thompson.—1st ed.
        p. cm.
    ISBN: 978-0-06-112392-4
    ISBN-10: 0-06-112392-7
    1. Baseball cards—Collectors and collecting—United States.   2. Baseball cards—United States—History.
    3. Wagner, Honus, 1874–1955.   I. Thompson, Teri.   II. Title.
GV875.3.O55 2007
796.357075—dc22

                                                        2006053078

07 08 09 10 11 WBC/RRD 10 9 8 7 6 5 4 3 2 1

To Lorna and Aidan, for all your love and support, and to Mom and Dad,
for teaching me to love the written word and baseball.
—Michael O'Keeffe

For Mom and Dad and the rest of the Thompson-Tinsley
clan—and, of course, Jim. Thank you.
—Teri Thompson

Special thanks to Nancy Thompson, editor par excellence.

CONTENTS

CONTENTS

THE CARD

PROLOGUE

The seeds of this book were planted on June 6, 2000, during a press conference at Mickey Mantle's, the Central Park South sports bar that's a favorite with tourists visiting New York City. On display for a small army of photographers and television cameramen, surrounded by a sea of sports photographs and autographed jerseys, was the Holy Grail of baseball collectibles, the most valuable and coveted trading card of all time—the T206 Honus Wagner PSA 8 NM-MT, also known as the Gretzky T206 Wagner.

Mastro Auctions Incorporated, the nation's biggest sports-memorabilia auction house (at the time it was known as Mastronet), had called the press conference to announce the sale of the ninety-one-year-old card in a special eBay auction, the first time the burgeoning online marketplace had joined in a venture with another auction house. The T206 Wagner, an undersize slice of cardboard featuring the rawboned Wagner in a stiff, high-collared "Pittsburg" jersey, would be offered on eBay later that year. Mastro executives said the bidding would begin at $500,000, and auction-house executive Robert Lifson predicted that the card could easily go for more than $1 million.

I am a reporter for the New York *Daily News,* and I had wandered over to Mantle's on that warm late-spring day looking for a good story and a sandwich. I found myself mesmerized as Mastro executives talked about a trading card in terms usually reserved for fine art; Lifson even proclaimed the Wagner "the Mona Lisa of all trading cards."

When the press conference ended, I approached Lifson as the restaurant staff cleared the tables and the TV crews packed away their gear. The card, shielded in a thick frame, appeared to be in terrific shape even though it had been printed in 1909—back when William Howard Taft was president, the automobile was still a rich man's toy, and Major League Baseball was a racially segregated game whose geographic reach ended in St. Louis.

I asked Lifson about the history of the card, and he repeated what had been said during the press conference. Most collectors recognize the T206 Wagner as the most desirable card in their hobby. It is a rare card—but by no means the hobby's rarest—because the American Tobacco Company, the cigarette manufacturer that issued the T206 series, abruptly stopped production of the card after Wagner refused to give permission to use his likeness.

Some people say that Wagner, still considered one of the game's greatest players, did not want to promote tobacco use to his young fans. Others say he was just another jock holding out for more money. Either way, an unknown number of T206 Wagners had already been printed and circulated in American Tobacco cigarette packs. Only a few dozen are known to have survived through the decades, and the Gretzky T206 Wagner is the ultimate catch, the most coveted and valuable T206 Wagner because of its superior condition.

The "PSA 8 NM-MT" in its name indicates that Professional Sports Authenticator—the Newport Beach, California, company that is the hobby's biggest and most important card authentication and grading service—has determined that the card is in near-mint to mint condition, an eight on a scale of one to ten. No other T206 Wagner even comes close. Its mystique is boosted by the fact that it was owned at one time by Wayne Gretzky, whose name graces the card.

The current owner, Lifson told me, was Michael Gidwitz, an affable Chicago investment adviser known for his extensive collection of original *Mad* magazine art. Gidwitz had purchased the Gretzky T206 Wagner four years earlier for a then-record $641,500 at an auction conducted by Christie's. The card had been consigned by Patricia Gibbs, a Florida postal worker who had won it in a contest sponsored by Wal-Mart. The retail giant had purchased the card, reportedly for more than $500,000, from Gretzky, the hockey legend known simply as "the Great One."

Lifson stopped and smiled, ready for my next question.

"You've only taken me back ten years," I said. "Where was this card for the first seventy years of its life? Where was this card during World War I? How did it survive the Great Depression? Who owned it when Neil Armstrong walked on the moon? And how can a piece of cardboard this old look this good?"

Lifson gave me a funny look. He seemed uncomfortable. Finally he said he didn't know.

The Gretzky T206 Wagner is the most valuable and the most famous trading card in the world. It has appeared with slugger Barry Bonds and Hall of Famer Brooks Robinson on CNN's *Larry King Weekend*, and it has been displayed at Major League Baseball's All-Star Game. It has been the headliner at national card shows, and it has presided over NASDAQ's opening-bell ceremony. It has been the focus of countless newspaper stories, trade-press articles, Internet posts, and television news reports.

It is the ultimate icon in what is known as "the hobby," a pastoral-sounding name for what was once a children's pastime and is now an unregulated and often cutthroat industry rife with fraud and corruption.

So why are there are all those gaping holes in its history? How did it survive wartime cardboard drives? Why wasn't it destroyed by bicycle spokes, damaged in a card-flipping marathon, or discarded by somebody's mother? How did the Gretzky T206 Wagner beat overwhelming odds to remain in near-mint condition almost a hundred years after it was printed? What's the big secret?

The Gretzky T206 Wagner is considered one of the great artifacts of baseball's long history, but, like so many of the scuffed balls, autographed bats, and stained jerseys that are held up as important and sold for big money by venerable auction houses and sports-collectibles Web sites, its origins and authenticity are riddled with questions and shrouded in mystery.

I asked Lifson how I could learn more about the card, and he told me to talk to Bill Mastro, the founder of Mastro Auctions and one of the most powerful men in the sports-collectibles industry. Mastro, Lifson told me, had "discovered" the card when he purchased it in 1985 for $25,000 from a small-time card collector on Long Island. Lifson failed to mention that he, too, was at the card shop when Mastro bought the Wagner, and that he even funded the transaction.

During that summer of 2000, a few weeks after the press conference at Mickey Mantle's, a Southern California businessman named Brian Seigel plunked down a whopping $1.265 million to buy the card from Gidwitz, and several months later (in the winter of 2001) I traveled to Bill Mastro's suburban Chicago office to interview him about the famous card.

Mastro is known in memorabilia circles as an aggressive, even ruthless, businessman, but he was warm and friendly when I walked into his headquarters in a suburban Oak Park office complex. He introduced me to his staff and we talked about some of his favorite pieces from his legendary collection. He owned autographed balls and game-used bats, an Old Gold cigarette ad from the 1930s featuring Babe Ruth, a cocktail napkin from Joe DiMaggio's restaurant on Fisherman's Wharf, an autographed studio portrait of Honus Wagner, and a Mr. Mets bobblehead doll. Heavyset and swaggering, with dark brown hair, a square jaw, and piercing eyes, he laughed as he talked about the old days, the days when he was young and crazy and would do just about anything to get his hands on a card he wanted.

"We were hungry maniacs," Mastro joked. "You would rather see a mad dog with froth coming out of his mouth than see one of us guys coming into your shop."

We sat down in his office to talk about the T206 Wagner he'd dragged out of obscurity and into the national spotlight some fifteen years earlier. The family of a printer, Mastro told me, had owned the card before he purchased it. He said he didn't remember much else.

I didn't know it at the time, but that meeting with Bill Mastro was the beginning of a quest for information that would endure for years. I began reporting on a burgeoning industry that few had examined in depth. Mastro stopped accepting my phone calls shortly after the *Daily News* published my story about the Gretzky T206 Wagner, but I have been writing about his auction house ever since our meeting in the winter of 2001.

Many in the media are reverential when it comes to vintage cards and game-used memorabilia. Echoing the collectors they write about, reporters regard the beat-up old gloves, sweaty jerseys, and ancient bats that now sell for hundreds of thousands of dollars as sacred relics, spiritual links to heroes of America's past, symbols of a simpler time. Others take a gee-whiz approach—isn't it kooky that someone would spend a million bucks on a baseball card? The fraud and deception are difficult to document, distasteful to pursue.

I dug deeper, began to cover the field of sports collectibles like the billion-dollar industry it is. The *Daily News* looked at how rare and valuable artifacts stolen from the Baseball Hall of Fame wound up for sale decades later in Mastro's auctions. We wrote about hobby insiders who inflate old bats and jerseys into priceless American artifacts once touched by Joe DiMaggio or Babe Ruth. We covered the hobby's top authenticators, self-anointed authorities with no real credentials whose opinions are openly mocked by trained experts and academics. We've written about professional athletes who supplement multimillion-dollar contracts by selling every cap and jockstrap they've ever worn on the game-used memorabilia market.

Some of our stories have upset the hobby's overlords and big collectors. Bill Mastro and Mastro Auctions president Doug Allen both declined to be interviewed for this book. So did Joe Orlando, the president of Professional Sports Authenticator, and Brian Seigel, a former owner of the Gretzky T206 Wagner. During one particularly long and angry phone call, Seigel berated me for not doing enough to promote the hobby; in his mind, no hint of scandal should touch his investment.

Only someone who has placed part of his fortune and his ego in sports collectibles could turn a blind eye to the hobby's many problems. During my winter 2001 interview with Bill Mastro, I told him about the rumor I'd heard, that there was a deep, dark secret behind the Gretzky T206 Wagner. I told Mastro I'd heard that the card had been restored. It was a serious allegation. Altering a T206 Wagner— or any other card—is like putting arms on the Venus de Milo. In the arcane world of trading cards, it is a serious infraction.

The Gretzky T206 Wagner didn't give up its secrets easily, nor did the men who have profited the most from it.

Mastro denied that the T206 has ever been restored and refused to discuss its provenance. He cursed a blue streak. Then he threw me out of his office.

—Michael O'Keeffe

EXPRESSWAY TO FORTUNE

The tension was as thick as the steel-gray clouds that hung over the Long Island Expressway as the beat-up old green Honda sped along on a Sunday evening in 1985, past the car washes and the billboards hard by the highway and into Hicksville, a New York City suburb built on the edges of what were once the potato fields that stretched into the far reaches of Long Island.

Bill Mastro and Rob Lifson weren't talking much as they drove into town from the Willow Grove card convention near Philadelphia to the doors of the collectibles shop in a dingy strip mall. The shop was closed to the public that day: Only Mastro and Lifson would be allowed in for a look at the treasure inside, and Lifson himself would barely get a glimpse, relegated to the front of the store while Mastro made the deal in the back.

What they found in the store that day would profoundly change both men's lives, even as it transformed the sleepy hobby of baseball-card collecting into a billion-dollar industry and turned an obsessive vintage-card collector into its most powerful player. It would ruin a friendship that had endured for years, and it would cast dark shadows over the hobby they both loved.

What they found in the store that day was The Card.

Jay Zimmerman was at the same convention in Willow Grove, Pennsylvania, in 1985 when he got the call from his pal Bob Sevchuk, the owner of a sports-collectibles store in Hicksville. Sevchuk could barely contain his excitement as he told Zimmerman about a regular customer who had come into the shop with a bounty of baseball cards. The man's name was Alan Ray, and Ray was eager to sell his wares, which included an outstanding T206 Honus Wagner card. Ray also had another rare and valuable card—a T206 Eddie Plank—as well as fifty to seventy-five other high-grade cards from the T206 series. This was like having a stranger walk into the local frame shop with a van Gogh, and Sevchuk knew that it was an opportunity for a big payday.

"Bob was selling it on consignment because he didn't want to lay out the money himself," Zimmerman said. "He asked me to approach people he knew who were into old cards."

Zimmerman's first stop at the show was Bill Mastro, then a thirty-three-year-old vintage-card connoisseur who had walked away from a career as a respiratory therapist just a few years earlier because he thought he could make more money selling cards and sports memorabilia. Mastro had been a fixture in the hobby since he was a teenager in Bernardsville, New Jersey, and he knew as much about old cards as anybody. Zimmerman told Mastro that Ray wanted $25,000 for a T206 Wagner card, an outrageous sum in those days even for the "Flying Dutchman." Mastro didn't flinch.

"You don't have to talk to anybody else," Mastro said. "I own it."

Mastro rounded up his old friend Lifson and told him he had a potential deal. They raced to Sevchuk's Long Island store with Lifson behind the wheel. "I got to go because I had the money," Lifson said. "I had no idea where we were going."

Mastro and Lifson had been friends for decades, bonding over their common zeal for trading cards and baseball memorabilia as boys. At twenty-five, the shaggy-haired Lifson was eight years younger than Mastro, a prodigy in the card-collecting hobby, a whiz kid who had begun dealing when he was ten years old. He and Mastro were buying, selling, and trading high-end cards before they could even shave, and their early partnership would help make both men formidable figures in the world of sports collectibles, eventual owners of two of the most prestigious sports auction houses in the world, Robert Edward Auctions and Mastro Auctions.

When he was barely in junior high, Lifson would track down Mastro at his college dorm in Bethlehem, Pennsylvania. Lifson was obsessed with baseball cards and with having a business built on them, and Mastro was just one of the many collectors he would routinely call on a daily basis.

"The monthly phone bill at our house was a big thing," Lifson said. "I'd call Bill all over the place. Someone would pick up the phone, and I'd say, 'Where can I reach him?' Bill has told a story for years about when I called and he's at a bar playing pool. The bartender says, 'Is there a Bill Mastro here?' "

Of course, it was Lifson. "No one told me I couldn't deal with adults," Lifson said.

When they arrived at Sevchuk's store that day, long before the wheels would come off their relationship, they found Sevchuk bursting with excitement. He whisked Mastro to the back of the store while Lifson waited up front examining the cards and collectibles in the display cases. "Bill instructed me to stay in front," Lifson said, "and Bill was like my customer, so I did that."

When Mastro returned with Sevchuk, the three of them discussed where the card had come from and how they might get others in similar condition from the same source. He showed Lifson the card briefly, then tucked it into a briefcase, locked the case, and they drove off.

Mastro had seen millions of cards by then, but he'd never seen a card like this Wagner. It was as if the heavens had parted and a divine hand delivered the Holy Grail of trading cards to a strip mall in Hicksville, New York. "Everything about it gives the appearance of, 'Holy Moses, this is too good to be true,'" Mastro would say years later.

It was a rare find, truly a one-of-a-kind piece, the sort of discovery most collectors only dream about. Mastro said it looked great for a seventy-five-year-old piece of cardboard, with no creases, tears, or blemishes. Even better, the back featured an advertisement for Piedmont cigarettes. Although dozens of T206 Wagners are still in circulation, almost all feature ads for Sweet Caporals, another brand of cigarettes. Only a handful of T206 Wagners have Piedmont backs.

Mastro was eager to buy the card, but he'd been collecting for more than twenty years and he knew how to keep his cool in the heat of a deal. He refused to complete the transaction unless Ray tossed in the fifty to seventy-five other T206 cards he'd brought to the shop in a shoe box, including a rare and valuable T206 Eddie Plank. The cards appeared to have been sliced from a printer's sheet—"you could almost cut yourself on the edges of some of the cards," Ray would say in a 2001 interview—the Wagner had wavy edges and a red printer's line at the top of the card, telling details that would not have escaped Mastro's keen eye. Mastro finally told Ray that the Wagner card "was not cut right, but I'll take it off your hands."

"I had a money situation," Ray said. "I had to sell the card."

Sevchuk and Ray have always been secretive about how Ray obtained the T206 Wagner or any of the other cards they sold to Mastro on that Sunday on Long Island in 1985. During a series of interviews in 2001, Ray was strangely evasive whenever the question came up; he said he got the card from a relative and had to obtain permission before he could identify the man. Several weeks later he moved from mysterious to confrontational: Ray said he was considering writing a book about his experiences with Mastro and the card.

"If I give you everything I know about the card, where does that leave me?" he asked.

Ray gave up what would become the world's most famous and valuable baseball card with barely a peep, and he is now the forgotten man in the story of the Gretzky T206 Wagner. Mastro appeared to have only vague memories of the man who sold him the card that would lay the foundation for his memorabilia empire. When he talked about Ray, he seemed to regard him as little more than a hiccup, a minor irritation in his quest for the card.

More than twenty years later, some hobby insiders still believe that Mastro bought the card from Sevchuk—Ray's name rarely emerges in discussions about its history. Mastro has told many people that he bought the card from the family of a printer, and that, too, has become part of the lore surrounding the Gretzky T206 Wagner.

Ray said he suspects that Mastro told people the story about the printer because he wanted to throw off anybody who tried to trace the provenance of the card.

"He bought it from me," Ray said. "There are no printers in my family."

The transaction took half an hour, maybe forty-five minutes, long enough for Lifson to grow bored with the cards in Sevchuk's glass cases. After Mastro let Lifson glimpse the card for just a few seconds, he continued his wheeling and dealing as soon as he and Lifson got back into the Honda. Rather than repay his friend the $25,000 in cash, Mastro suggested he give Lifson a lesser quality T206 Wagner from his personal collection. Lifson could sell the card for $30,000 and make a tidy $5,000 profit. Lifson was doubtful: Who would pay $30,000 for such a baseball card?

"The price was so much, just too much for a card," Lifson said. "It wouldn't matter if Wagner could walk, talk, and clean the house—it was too much."

But he was convinced that Bill Mastro understood how rich and obsessed collectors think, and that his friend knew how to make a buck.

"I wasn't that comfortable with that arrangement, because we were talking about a lot of money," Lifson said. "But there was a built-in insurance policy, because Bill was involved. No matter what, he'd be good for it."

Lifson was right to put aside his misgivings. Within a week he would sell the card Mastro had given him to Barry Halper for $30,000. Halper, the New Jersey businessman who at one time was a limited partner in George Steinbrenner's New York Yankees ownership group, is best known for his massive sports-memorabilia collection that ranged from the truly historic (Shoeless Joe Jackson's Black Betsey bat) to the truly bizarre (Ty Cobb's dentures and the rifle Cobb's mother used to shoot his father).

There may never be another collector like Halper, the Babe Ruth of sports memorabilia who died in 2005 at age sixty-six from complications of diabetes. He acquired his first piece when he was eight years old, hanging outside the players' gate at Newark's minor-league Bears Stadium. A player named Barney McCosky gave him a jersey, and, like a hungry cub, Halper kept going back to ballparks for more, pestering players for old balls, gloves, and bats. Halper eventually amassed a huge, hundred-thousand-piece collection, and his Livingston, New Jersey, home—dubbed "Cooperstown South"—featured a computerized dry-cleaning rack he used to store the 1,068 uniforms he'd picked up over the years.

He later said that collecting memorabilia was his way of getting close to the players and the game he loved, and in the course of a relentless decades-long pursuit of baseball artifacts, he developed friendships with some of the game's greatest names, including Joe DiMaggio, Ted Williams, Yogi Berra, Bob Feller, Pete Rose, and Phil Rizzuto. At the 1994 press conference to announce his successful liver transplant, Mickey Mantle spotted Halper in the audience and yelled out, "Hey, Barry, did you get my other liver?"

In 1998, Major League Baseball gave Halper $5 million for the T206 Wagner he had purchased from Lifson and for two hundred other baseball artifacts he had acquired over fifty years. MLB donated the cache to the Baseball Hall of Fame in the real Cooperstown. The bulk of the Halper collection, however, was sold for more than $25 million in 1999 at a historic Sotheby's auction that was overseen by Lifson. (Even in death Halper amazed the collectibles world. In September 2006, Lifson would auction thirty balls from Halper's estate featuring the somewhat shocking inscription from Rose: "I'm sorry I bet on baseball—Pete Rose.")

The Halper auction remains the greatest single event in the history of sports collectibles, and it was certainly one of the high points of Lifson's career. The auction earned him a reputation as a powerful auctioneer who could write an enormous catalog, organize lots, massage wealthy but high-maintenance collectors, and handle a massive sale that had garnered international attention.

"It really doesn't get any better than that from our perspective," Lifson said. "I felt like Babe Ruth and it was 1927."

But in 1985, as he drove Mastro back to the airport, Lifson could barely envision what would come of the business he'd gotten into as a ten-year-old kid. All he knew was that, unlike other collectors of the day, Mastro was obsessed with the condition of his cards and that he'd picked up a beauty that day. He also knew that Mastro had been willing to pay an absurd amount for it. Alan Ray would say later that Mastro and Lifson "knew what they were going to do with this card," but Lifson wouldn't see the card again for years, not until it had been slabbed between two sheets of plastic and graded, labeled the most valuable baseball card in the world.

That day, in his old green Honda, Lifson could not even dream of what would become of the card he'd financed. But Bill Mastro had already hatched a plan for it.

KING OF THE HILL

The story behind the Gretzky T206 Wagner can't be told without telling the story of Bill Mastro.

The card's skyrocketing price tag has paralleled and stoked the rise of sports collectibles from eccentric hobby to big business, and Mastro has been with it every step of the way. Not only did Mastro lift the Gretzky T206 Wagner out of obscurity and into the international spotlight, but he has played a role—as a buyer, seller, bidder, or auctioneer—almost every time The Card has changed hands.

In many ways he is the George Steinbrenner of his industry. Like the New York Yankees' owner, Mastro is a hot-tempered perfectionist, a blunt and hard-nosed businessman who seems incapable of settling for second place. And as with Steinbrenner, nobody feels ambivalent about Bill Mastro: People either love him or hate him.

"Bill is a very powerful personality," Lifson said. "He is a larger-than-life figure, and a lot of people want to be his buddy. He's always had this grand vision. Bill has always looked to do things in a big, big way. Along the way, he has also made a lot of people very angry."

Or as Mastro himself puts it, "If you add up the number of people I've irritated, it would be a lot."

The auction house he founded, Mastro Auctions, is a monster in the sports-collectibles world; his Burr Ridge, Illinois, company does twice as much business as Leland's, its nearest competitor. Mastro views the competition with an arrogant disdain. "The others are all dinosaurs," he once said. "They're greedy pigs."

In recent years Mastro Auctions has expanded into the Americana, comic-book, and fine-art markets. It even considered getting into finance: Mastro executives have talked about creating a division that would offer memorabilia insurance and loans to collectors. The company's bread and butter, though, has always been sports collectibles, baseball cards in particular, and Mastro Auctions has played a role in the purchase and sale of some of the most famous sports memorabilia in history.

The $1.265 million Seigel paid for the Gretzky T206 Wagner in 2000 was the highest price ever for a baseball card and one of the highest for a sports-related collectible. (Tops is the $3.05 million that *Spawn* creator Todd McFarlane paid at a 1999 Guernsey's Auction for Mark McGwire's seventieth-home-run ball from the 1998 season.)

When Mastro began his business in the 1980s, he had little more than a mobile phone and the trunk of his car. Now he has thirty employees who helped pull in $45 million in auction revenue in 2005 (up $5 million from 2004). But Mastro's influence in the hobby goes far beyond dollars and cents. Mastro was just a kid, a twelve-year-old Mets fan from rural Bernardsville, New Jersey, when he first plunged into collecting. Back then, in the mid-1960s, it was a loose network of men and even boys who swapped baseball cards through mimeographed newsletters and tiny classified ads in the backs of sports magazines. Candy stores sold the latest issues from Topps, of course, but collectors had to be committed if they wanted to pursue older cards. There were no card shows, hobby shops, or Internet sites where collectors could purchase vintage cards. These could be obtained from dealers or other collectors, but negotiations were usually conducted by mail, and deals could take weeks—even months—to complete.

"Some of my best friends in the hobby I never even met in person," said legendary collector Bill Heitman, the Southern California attorney who authored *The Monster*, a definitive guide to the T206 series. "Long-distance phone calls were expensive then. People were letter writers."

Bill Mastro helped changed all that. He is one of the people who turned sports memorabilia and trading cards—"the hobby"—into a $2-billion-a-year Internet-driven industry that has several regional trade shows every month and a national convention that has drawn more than a hundred thousand sports fans over a summer weekend. Mastro wasn't the first to apply the business model refined by fine-art auction houses like Sotheby's and Christie's to sports collectibles; Josh Evans gave what had previously been a hobby conducted out of automobile trunks and hotel rooms a sense of gravitas when he founded Lelands in 1987. The hobby's first "celebrity," meanwhile, was Al Rosen, a tireless self-promoter known as "Mr. Mint" who got a lot of attention by purchasing full-page ads in hobby publications and literally flashing wads of cash at collectors who passed his booth at card conventions.

But in the decades that have passed, Mastro has catapulted to the head of the pack, and he is now one of the most powerful men in sports collectibles. There are numerous reasons for his success: Many top collectors praise Mastro Auctions because they claim it consistently offers high-quality pieces, superior customer service, and a knowledgeable staff. Consignors get top prices for their cards and collectibles. (Auction houses charge buyers and sellers a commission, so they profit from those high prices, too.) Mastro's catalogs, with their splendid color photography and flowery text, have become collectors' items in their own right. They look like expensive coffee-table books and are distributed to twenty thousand high-roller collectors, professional athletes, sports executives, and museums several times a year.

Perhaps most important, Mastro's was the first house to offer auction bidders a secure and easy-to-use Internet site. Mastronet .com receives roughly 3 million hits during each of its auctions, making it the hobby's most popular Web site.

"Bill wasn't the first at a lot of things," Evans said. "But he took the auction business one step further than everybody else."

Mastro sold his auction house in late 2004 to SilkRoad Equity, a private investment firm owned by high-tech entrepreneur Andrew "Flip" Filipowski, the ponytailed businessman who founded divine Inc., an Internet empire that became synonymous in Chicago business circles with high-tech excess after the company burned through $1 billion of investors' money before it went bankrupt in 2003. Mastro, however, remains the auction house's CEO, and he is still deeply involved in its nuts-and-bolts operation. "I'm not like some other executives who sit behind a desk and oversee things," Mastro said in 2005. "I have conversations with each one of our employees every day, no matter where I am. I'm down in the trenches. I personally go through collections. I personally load things on trucks."

But there are others who rip through the hyperbole and the accolades and cut to the chase. Michael Gidwitz, the Chicago investment adviser and former owner of the Gretzky T206 Wagner, has known Mastro since the days of the card shows in the seventies, when they would meet in the hotel rooms and lodge halls to pore over old Topps and Goudey sets.

Gidwitz had known Mastro through big transactions and minor

deals, but in recent years their relationship has soured. He said he has overpaid for some items and had some rejected by other auction houses as having been doctored. He cited a 1947 Jackie Robinson advertising plaque that he bought from Mastro for $3,300 and then could sell for only $1,044, and a Chicago Cubs display piece called "Yard of the Cubs" he said was rejected at auction for having been altered.

A collector of the caliber of Gidwitz is appalled by what the hobby has become, by the "card doctors," who buy old cards, fix them up, and resell them for more money.

Restoration work is widely accepted for fine art or antiques, a common practice among even the most famous paintings. But a baseball-card dealer who admits that a card has been altered shoots himself in the foot. For most collectors the ideal card has not been altered since it was slipped out of the package of cigarettes, tobacco, or gum years before. Cards that have been trimmed, colored, or repaired are considered tainted and are worth considerably less.

Professional Sports Authenticator, a division of a company called Collectors Universe, was born in 1991 to protect collectors from card doctors, counterfeiters, and other cheats. Several other major grading firms—Sportscard Guaranty Corporation, Beckett Grading Services, and Global Authentication Incorporated—followed, and like PSA they advertised themselves as sheriffs who brought law and order to a Wild West industry. PSA, however, remained the hobby's dominant grading company, its most prestigious name, its gold standard.

The value of a trading card is based primarily on condition and content. Mickey Mantle, of course, will always be more valuable than Horace Clarke. Cards with asymmetrical borders, faded coloring, fuzzy printing, curled corners, pinholes, creases, tears, gum stains, and other blemishes can be worth hundreds of thousands of dollars less than the same card in better condition. A few months after Brian Seigel paid $1.265 million for the near-mint to mint Gretzky card, another Wagner—this one graded PSA 1, in poor to fair condition—sold for a measly $50,935. That difference in price, obviously, makes the temptation to repair and restore cards quite compelling.

"Doctoring is the biggest issue we have to deal with," said Beckett Grading Service's grader Andy Broome. "The higher in value a card is, the more susceptible it is to being doctored."

As the value of cards skyrocketed in the 1980s, card doctors stepped in to breathe new life into tired old specimens. It is easy to imagine them, wild-eyed, with razor blades and scalpels, plying their trade in dark basements, fumbling with their test tubes until bright, shiny new creations emerge. Their techniques range from the obviously simple to the surprisingly sophisticated. Some procedures are less objectionable than others to collectors. Nylon stockings, for example, can be rubbed on a card to remove stains left by bubble gum or wax packaging, and many collectors find that within the limits of acceptability. A much smaller number approve of using the back of a spoon to smooth out creases and wrinkles. And shaving off dirty edges with a razor blade or a nail file is taboo: For most collectors it is not acceptable to add or subtract anything from a card to bolster its value.

Sometimes cards are flattened with vises, bricks or, books—if the cardboard can be compressed and stretched even a little, poor-quality edges and corners can be trimmed even as the card remains within accepted size parameters. Another trick is combining two cards—putting together the back of one card with the front of another to create a Frankenstein card worth much more than the sum of its parts.

Some dealers even use laser cutters to trim their cards. "A laser cutter can cost $8,000 or more, and that may sound like a lot of money," Beckett's Andy Broome said. "But the difference between a card that's graded a seven and an eight can be even more than that. A laser cutter could pay for itself with one card."

Graphic Conservation, a Chicago company that restores art and historic documents for museums and collectors, first dry-cleans cards to eliminate stains and debris. Cards with creases and wrinkles are put into high-pressure presses. Flabby corners are built up with wheat starch. Holes are filled with paper pulp. Mastro Auctions is one of Graphic Conservation's best card-restoration customers.

"Some people are passionate about cards and want their cards to look their best," office manager William Bengtson said. "Other people want work done so they can improve the resale value. We understand this can be controversial, but we make no moral judgments. We do tell collectors they are walking a fine line."

Lifson is obsessed with the issue of card doctoring and what it has done to the collectibles industry, even though he can barely keep up with the technology. It used to be that an expert like Lifson could spot a fraud a mile away—and if he couldn't detect it with the naked eye, he'd put it under a black light that would reveal corners repaired with wheat starch and holes filled with paper pulp, making them practically glow.

"It used to be that simple," he said. "We bought a black light at Home Depot. If it's glowing, you know the area has restoration."

A set of 1957 Topps cards that had been consigned to one of his recent auctions, Lifson said, was purchased at a 1992 Sotheby's auction for $13,000. The consignor was unaware that the cards had been altered. "They should have been the best set in the world," Lifson said. "Fact was, every single card had been doctored. All built up by professional restorers. I had to tell the guy."

Lifson wound up putting the cards in the auction as doctored, and, to his surprise, the seller got real money for them—$3,750—even though he took a considerable loss. Lifson can't help but point out that Mastro was the "expert" (someone hired by the auction house to deal with the authentication process, write catalog descriptions, and deal with consignors) working for Sotheby's when those cards were sold in 1992.

Card alteration has become so commonplace and the problem so widespread, in fact, that Lifson's company has staked out the moral high ground in its advertising, positioning itself as the company that doesn't cheat. The cards go out of Lifson's auction house in exactly the same condition they came in.

In April 2006, Robert Edward Auctions sent out this mass e-mail to its customers:

> Many serious dealers and collectors are particularly enthused about the opportunity to bid on cards at Robert Edward Auctions, not just because the material is great, but for another reason that is rarely openly discussed: We don't "do anything" to the cards. Robert Edward Auctions does not file the edges or corners of cards, "squash" cards, press cards, bleach cards, re-back cards, restore cards, clean cards, trim cards, remove creases or in any other way doctor or alter any card.
>
> This is in marked contrast to common practices which buyers encounter elsewhere at times. Some establishments as a routine part of their business model have cards "worked on" on a regular basis, even employing people whose primary responsibilities specifically include altering cards (many or most of which are owned by the company). One of our biggest auction buyers in recent years has been one of our many competitors who has spent six figures purchasing graded cards from our auctions, breaking them out of their

holders, working on them, getting them regraded and offering them again at auction.

Lifson fears that altered cards will destroy the hobby, and there is little he can do to stop it, particularly with the sophisticated methods of card doctors.

"I'm not a scientist," he said. "I'm a guy with a black light in the bathroom."

Perhaps the biggest reason for Bill Mastro's success is his ability to charm the community of wealthy male collectors—the movie director Penny Marshall is one of the few women in the sports collectible world with an extensive collection—who have the money and inclination to drop $50,000 or more on old baseball cards. Some of these collectors are like the medieval Christians who built cathedrals around the knucklebone of a long-dead saint. They'll spend a fortune for a card they believe provides them some link to their childhood heroes and the sport they grew up venerating.

Others use the hobby for prestige and approval. "They think they are important people because they own a Joe DiMaggio bat or a T206 Wagner," one East Coast collector said. "They have a hole in their psyche they need to fill by owning the very best. Bill understands the psychology of those collectors and uses it to his advantage."

Mastro knows how to talk to them. He has an uncanny ability to find a baseball card or another collectible that satisfies their emotional cravings, their spiritual hungers, those "holes in their psyche."

By 1987, when Mastro found the perfect buyer for his perfect T206 Wagner, its condition was nearly flawless.

Jim Copeland, the well-heeled owner of a sporting-goods chain based in San Luis Obispo, California, was a hobby unknown who had a reputation for paying too much for cards and memorabilia. Copeland, seemingly overnight, built an impressive collection with the help of card dealer Greg Bussineau, and he told Bussineau he wanted to purchase a T206 Wagner.

Copeland was a high-powered businessman, well dressed and sophisticated, and Bussineau knew that his client would need access to the best merchandise out there—and he also knew who owned the best T206 Wagner in the world. "It was in immaculate shape," according to Bussineau. "It's hard to believe they can stay in that shape for so many years."

"Jim was a good customer," Bussineau added. "I knew Bill had the card, so I told him I have a gentleman interested in buying it."

Copeland had already read an article about Mastro, and he was impressed with the rising collectibles star. By that time Mastro and Bussineau had flown to California to meet with Copeland, and Mastro had become quite impressed with Copeland—and his money—too.

Soon Mastro was counseling Copeland on the finer points of the hobby. Mastro emphasized to Copeland that appearance was the most important thing to consider when buying cards—cards that are aesthetically pleasing would command top dollar when it came time to sell them. Copeland was willing to pay through the nose for cards in excellent condition, and for $110,000 he purchased the card Alan Ray had sold to Mastro for $25,000. Bussineau received a $10,000 commission. Mastro pocketed the rest.

It was a sale that would revolutionize card collecting. The price of T206 Wagners, which had been retreating in value, suddenly escalated. So did the price tag for all kinds of cards.

"Copeland changed everything. He created an incentive to sell these great cards. It's not like the card ever sold for $50,000 or $75,000," said Lifson, who sold Copeland cards from his personal collection in 1990. "It went from $25,000 to $110,000 overnight, with nothing in between."

That sale established Mastro as one of the hobby's top dealers, one of the men who could provide the rich and the obsessive with the very best. Selling his Gretzky T206 Wagner didn't make Mastro's career—even his biggest enemies say the guy is so smart and so driven that he would have been successful without it. But the sale to Copeland put him on the map as a dealer to watch.

Mastro, however, probably wasn't thinking that far down the line after he completed the sale to Copeland.

"I called from the airport in California," Mastro said, "and I ordered a Mercedes-Benz."

3

TOBACCO ROAD

In 1910 an astounding 10 billion cigarettes were made in the United States, most by the American Tobacco Company (ATC), which manufactured just about every cigarette on the market under brands such as American Beauty, Carolina Brights, Cycle, El Principe de Gales, Hindu, Piedmont, and Sweet Caporal. The typical pack contained ten cigarettes and one card. The Honus Wagner was among the 524 cards depicting players from the National League and the upstart American League, formed just a few years earlier in 1901. Players from several minor leagues were also included in the series, an attempt to market the brands in the South and the West long before Major League Baseball expanded to the Sun Belt. The T206 series is so much bigger than other tobacco card sets—its closest rival, the T205 series, has just 209 cards—that Bill Heitman dubbed it "the Monster."

Baseball cards, of course, had been around for many years before the T206 series was issued. Most historians trace their advent to the 1880s, when cards were first mass-produced and distributed nationwide. Cards portraying baseball in some fashion date back decades earlier, however, even if they didn't provide player stats or come with bubble gum. Baseball historian Hank Thomas and his partners Frank Ceresi and Kevin Keating displayed what they called the earliest known baseball card at a July 2005 Smithsonian Institution symposium on the history of trading cards; the card was also displayed at the National Sports Collectors Convention that summer. This card was apparently used in some type of children's game, and Thomas believes that it was printed sometime between 1800 and 1830, when baseball was still evolving into what would become America's national pastime. It featured an illustration of a boy pitching a ball to another kid who is holding what appears to be a bat. Another boy stands at what might be first base. "Boys delight with ball to play," the caption says.

"This is the only card that shows the origins of baseball," said Thomas, the great turn-of-the-century pitcher Walter Johnson's grandson and biographer. Johnson and Wagner were members of the first Hall of Fame class, inducted in 1936. "It is the only card I'm aware of that captures the period when the game was developing."

As baseball became an increasingly important part of American life in the years before the Civil War, fans began collecting and trading baseball-themed cards. The larger versions of these cards were called "cabinet cards," because they were intended for display in cabinets. Smaller cards were known as "cartes de visite," or calling cards, and they were distributed to friends and family during parties and other social events. They might feature a portrait of the bearer but could also portray family members, actors, animals, political figures, or athletes. Baseball was an especially popular theme, and many of these cards—really just photographs pasted onto a cardboard backing—featured local baseball clubs or young boys wearing baseball uniforms. Some, however, depicted well-known players and teams.

Unlike modern cards, these were considered personal mementos. The first baseball cards mass-produced for commercial purposes appeared in New York City during the 1860s; a sporting-goods company named Peck & Snyder distributed "trade cards" on street corners. A picture of a famous player or team appeared on one side of the card, while an advertisement for Peck & Snyder "Base Ball and Sports Man's Emporium" graced the other. The Cincinnati Red Stockings, the first professional baseball club (later known simply as the Reds), appeared on a Peck & Snyder card in 1869, seven years before the formation of the National League. Robert Edward Auctions sold one described as "excellent" at its April 2006 sale for $2,200.

Thanks to Peck & Snyder's success, other companies followed suit in the 1870s and 1880s. Trade cards also spawned a new hobby: card collecting. The cards, some of which featured scenes such as the one in which a young girl tells a visitor, "Of course I'm a good girl—my father calls me a holy terror," weren't particularly funny but were a hit with Victorian-era collectors. People spent countless evenings pasting new acquisitions onto the pages of their scrapbooks or showing off their collection to their friends. By the 1880s, collecting trade cards was the fashionable thing to do.

The first baseball cards modern fans would recognize appeared in that decade, when cigarette companies issued twenty-five-card sets. The companies used the cards to advertise their products, build brand loyalty, and promote cigarettes to future generations (smokers, after all, often gave the cards to their children). One added benefit: The cards stiffened packs, protecting cigarettes from bending or breaking during shipping.

Goodwin & Company of New York, the manufacturer of Old Judge, Gypsy Queen, Dogs Head, and other cigarette brands, issued a twelve-card set in 1886 that included future Hall of Famers Roger Conner, Tim Keefe, and Buck Ewing. A Virginia tobacco company, Allen & Ginter, followed up the next year with a fifty-card set that featured ten baseball players as well as "sports" figures such as Wild West Show star Annie Oakley and the boxer John Sullivan. Goodwin & Company fired back between 1887 and 1890 with a huge set now known as the "Old Judge series" that pictured more than five hundred ballplayers in a variety of poses.

Then the American Tobacco Company came along and nearly killed off cards during the 1890s, after James Buchanan "Buck" Duke convinced four other leading cigarette manufacturers—Allen & Ginter, Goodwin & Company, the F. S. Kinney Company, and William S. Kimball & Company—to merge in 1889 with his W. Duke & Sons & Company. By the early 1890s, the new company—the American Tobacco Company—had become a monopoly and, because it faced little competition, raised prices and slashed what it deemed unnecessary costs. Advertising and sales promotions were no longer required. Baseball cards appeared to be on the road to extinction.

Duke later extended his empire into cigars and plug tobacco, creating a trust that controlled all three major areas of the tobacco industry. This was the era of President Theodore Roosevelt, the trustbuster whose administration filed lawsuits against Standard Oil, U.S. Steel, and dozens of other companies, aimed at breaking up monopolies and promoting competition. In 1907 the government began legal action to ease Duke's grip on tobacco.

ATC was feeling nervous by 1909, and, perhaps not coincidentally, baseball cards reappeared in tobacco packaging. The heat wasn't coming just from the government: Upstart companies that manufactured cigarettes made of exotic tobacco blends imported from Turkey also threatened the monopoly's market grip. ATC turned to the national pastime for help. A single T206 card was inserted into packs containing ten cigarettes as a way to lure baseball fans to buy the company's brands. In 1911 the U.S. Supreme Court ordered the

Duke tobacco trust dissolved, but Buck Duke's sports legacy didn't end with T206 cards. Just before his death in 1925, Duke created a $40 million endowment. The chief beneficiary was a North Carolina school then known as Trinity College, which later became the college basketball powerhouse Duke University.

The T206 series has always been popular with collectors. One reason is that the series features an incredible roster: The T206 set includes more than seventy players now enshrined in the Baseball Hall of Fame, including three members of Cooperstown's inaugural class—Wagner, Ty Cobb, and Walter Johnson. (Legendary pitcher Cy Young and Wagner's teammate/manager Fred Clarke are also featured in the set.) But much of the credit must go to the cards themselves—gorgeously illustrated portraits printed in vibrant colors. Most of the studio portraits—including the iconic Wagner head-and-shoulders shot—were taken in the Boston studio of Carl Horner, one of baseball's prominent turn-of-the-century photographers.

The cards were printed at seven factories in New York, Ohio, Virginia, and North Carolina. The factory where each card was made was stamped on the back. The Gretzky T206 Wagner was imprinted with "Factory 25, 24 Dist. Va.," indicating that the Wagner cards were made at Factory 25 in Virginia. According to T206 historian Scot A. Reader, the vast majority of the Piedmont cards and cigarettes were made at Factory 25.

A typical card is 1⁷⁄₁₆ by 2⅝ inches, but the size of T206 cards can vary widely, which would later fuel rumors that many of them are altered. Oversize cards, of course, give card doctors ample room to trim rounded corners and dirty edges and thereby improve appearance. "It is not at all uncommon to find T206 examples that have been altered at some point during their near-century of existence," Reader wrote in his *Inside T206: A Collector Guide to the Classic Baseball Card Set.*

Based on a 1915 U.S. government report on the tobacco industry, Reader estimated that as many as 370 million T206 cards were produced between 1909 and 1911. Although they were printed on heavy, durable paper stock, only a fraction still exist. "First, T206 cards were distributed as a premium rather than as a primary product," explained Reader, a Colorado patent attorney. "Most early-1900s cigarette purchasers were interested in a smoke, not a small cardboard insert depicting a baseball player. As painful as it is to ponder for those of us who love T206, tens of millions of T206 specimens were probably discarded without so much as an initial viewing.

"Second, T206 cards were distributed to an adult population. Most adults are far less interested in saving novelty items than [are] kids. Third, baseball cards had no economic value at the time. There was accordingly no economic incentive to keep them."

Count in all the hazards trading cards face on an almost-daily basis—paper drives, dirty-fingered kids, spring cleanings, house fires, basement floods—and it's amazing that so many T206 cards are still around. Reader estimated that 1.6 million remain in circulation, but this, like so much else about the T206 series, he admits is just speculation. "This is quite possibly less than one percent of the original production, with the vast majority of these survivors being in lower grade," he said.

The T206 Wagner isn't the only extremely rare card in the series. Another card that has long frustrated collectors is the T206 card of Philadelphia A's pitcher Eddie Plank. (One of the cards Mastro picked up from Alan Ray in Hicksville, in fact, was a Plank card that he later sold for $3,000 to $4,000. Another Plank sold at the Halper Auction for $18,000.) According to Lifson, the Plank lacks the "story" that comes with the Wagner, although some say that Plank, like Wagner, objected to the use of his image on a tobacco card.

Some have suggested that the Hall of Famer's T206 scarcity is the result of a broken printing plate. Nobody knows for sure, but Reader estimated there may be fewer than a hundred Plank cards still in circulation.

Another rarity is Sherry Magee's misspelled T206 card. Magee was one of the National League's best hitters for years, but that apparently didn't impress the printers who identified him as "Magie" on an early run of portrait cards. The mistake was eventually caught and corrected; one hundred to two hundred of the error cards have survived. Two other rare cards were printed after the players were traded. Giants outfielder Bill O'Hara was traded to the St. Louis Cardinals, and Ray Demmitt was shipped by the New York Highlanders to the Browns after the 1909 season, but most of their cards feature their old teams.

Then there is "Slow Joe" Doyle's extremely rare T206. Doyle, a pitcher with the New York Highlanders (an early incarnation of the Yankees), is featured in a more common version bearing a team caption that identifies him as a player for "N.Y." A nearly impossible-to-obtain version, however, says he played with "N.Y. Nat'l." Reader said the factory may have confused "Slow Joe" with "Laughing Larry" Doyle of the New York Giants. Whatever the reason, the Doyle error card may be the T206 series's most elusive trophy. Only a dozen or so are known to still exist, and they command top dollar, but because Wagner was a much better player and because his card has a better backstory, the ultra-rare T206 Doyle mistake card fetches a fraction of the Wagner. In 2000 one Doyle sold for $179,000 at a Ron Oser Auction, then a division of Mastronet.

Honus Wagner was at the peak of his career in 1909, and that made him a natural for inclusion in the T206 set. The Pittsburgh Pirates beat the Detroit Tigers in the World Series to conclude the 1909 season, and Wagner was widely hailed as the game's greatest player. He performed magnificently in the World Series—.333 batting average, six stolen bases, stellar defensively. His rival Ty Cobb, the American League's contender for the best-player title, hit a paltry .231 for the defeated Tigers. Wagner's Pirates slumped in 1910, finishing the season in third place, but Wagner was still the National League's biggest name.

By 1910, Wagner's likeness had already appeared on a few products, including chewing gum, baseball gear, soft drinks, beer, ice cream, analgesic balm, even gunpowder. Some of the companies never bothered to ask for his consent. Others paid him a token amount. In 1909, endorsements were not all that lucrative for athletes, and Wagner never expressed much enthusiasm for any of the products that bore his name or likeness.

But Wagner reacted swiftly and surely to a Pittsburgh sportswriter named John Gruber, who had been hired by the American Tobacco Company to obtain Wagner's permission to use his likeness on cards that would be distributed in several brands. According to an article in the October 12, 1912, issue of the *Sporting News*, Gruber's letter to Wagner prompted a strong rebuke. Wagner told the sportswriter he did not want his picture packaged with cigarettes and threatened to take legal action if American Tobacco proceeded. Almost a hundred years later, there are two schools of thought addressing Wagner's reluctance to sign on. Did he reject the deal because he wanted to protect young fans from the evils of tobacco? Or was he just another jock holding out for more money?

The cynical camp's position has been forcefully argued by broadcaster Keith Olbermann, the anchor of MSNBC's *Countdown*, who is widely respected as a collector and vintage card scholar. Wagner, Olbermann and his allies like to point out, enjoyed tobacco. He was a cigar aficionado. He liked to chew at the ballpark, and there are many photos showing him with a clump of chaw in his mouth.

"I remember sitting with him in a large chair," said Wagner's granddaughter Leslie Blair, who was five years old when her grandfather died in 1955. "He was always chewing tobacco."

Wagner, moreover, had appeared on a cigar trading card more than a decade earlier. Cigar makers in Pittsburgh and Louisville (where he played before he joined the Pirates) had sold stogies with Wagner's face on the box. During the 1909 World Series, Pittsburgh newspapers featured ads with a Wagner action pose for Murad cigarettes. "A hit every time," the ad read.

Another reason Olbermann and his allies may be right: Wagner was known as a tough negotiator in an era when many players, often poorly educated, hammered out their own contracts with team lawyers and executives, and it would not have been out of character for him to have played hardball when it came to money. In December 1907, for example, Wagner announced his retirement, telling fans that injuries and advanced age (the Flying Dutchman was thirty-three years old) had simply worn him out. Big-league baseball back then was a much more brutal game than it is today. Base runners spiked and kicked infielders; infielders punched and kicked base runners. During the 1909 World Series against the American League Detroit Tigers, according to what may be more legend than reality, Wagner either bloodied Ty Cobb's lip or knocked out a couple of teeth in a hard tag after Cobb announced, "I'm coming down on the next pitch, Krauthead," before attempting to steal second base. Baseball was indeed a hard life: Teams traveled long distances on dirty, loud, coal-powered trains, ate cheap food, and slept in rough hotels.

But the "retirement" lasted until just after the start of the 1908 season, when Wagner signed a contract for $10,000—a 100 percent increase over his 1907 salary and almost two hundred times what the average American earned. Wagner always swore that his 1907 retirement announcement was sincere. Still, he didn't leave the game until 1917, at forty-three.

In an age when athletes regularly make headlines for steroids, rape allegations, and murder charges, it is tempting to view the antitobacco theory as naive and quaint. An athlete who isn't a self-absorbed millionaire, a ballplayer who actually cares about his fans? Preposterous! There is, however, one serious flaw to the cynical camp's theory. The *Sporting News* story reported that Wagner sent a check for $10 to Gruber to compensate for the fee ATC would have paid the sportswriter if Wagner had signed on. If Wagner were holding out for more money, why would he send $10—a considerable amount of money in 1909—to Gruber? (Gruber, perhaps sports memorabilia's first check collector, never cashed the check. He saved and framed it.)

Moreover, the truth may be much more complicated than proponents of the antismoking school acknowledge. It's not hard to speculate about what was going on in Wagner's head when he received that letter from John Gruber. By 1909, Wagner, the son of a coal-mining German immigrant, had become a man to be reckoned with in western Pennsylvania. He was the best and most popular player in baseball, and he was already building a life away from the diamond. Wagner had invested in a number of business ventures in his hometown of Carnegie. He also had a growing interest in politics, and candidates throughout Pennsylvania courted him for his endorsement. While Wagner took great interest in Republican Party issues, GOP leaders tried but failed to convince him to run for several elected posts.

Wagner, in other words, was a respectable man, and in 1909, respectable people did not smoke cigarettes. Decades later a butt would dangle from the mouth of every movie hero, every rock star, every rebel without a cause, but before World War I, cigarettes—especially the nickel packs popular with laborers—were considered low-class and, even then, a threat to the public health. The cigar was a symbol of prosperity and accomplishment. Chew and pipe tobacco were safe and traditional. But in 1900, cigarettes were illegal in fourteen states. The Supreme Court called them a "noxious" product.

"A belief in their deleterious effects, particularly among young people, has become very general," the court said in 1900 when it upheld Tennessee's prohibition on cigarette sales (this at a time when opium and heroin were available over the counter).

In addition, the two men most responsible for Wagner's on-field and off-field success—Pirates manager Fred Clarke and owner Barney Dreyfuss—both despised cigarettes. Dreyfuss even passed on a chance to sign a young Tris Speaker because Speaker smoked. (Despite the cigarettes, Speaker went on to have a Hall of Fame career.) So it seems likely that the ambitious Wagner would have wanted to avoid associating with something that made reputable people uneasy.

Wagner, moreover, respected his fans, especially the young ones. He had a reputation in Pittsburgh as a star who would hold the player gate open a tad longer than necessary so kids could slip into the ballpark behind him for free. "He loved children," granddaughter Blair said. "He wanted to teach kids good sportsmanship. When it came time for that card to come out, it wasn't that he wasn't paid. He didn't want kids to have to buy tobacco to get his card."

The Wagner T206, Scot Reader added, might be much more common if the American Tobacco Company had played hardball with Wagner. A letter sent by New York sportswriter and ATC rep

Bozeman Bulger to Highlanders shortstop Neal Ball says that the company needed Ball's permission for inclusion in the T206 series "under a new law they have here." (Ball apparently gave his okay, since he appears in the set.) Reader believes that Bulger was likely referring to the New York Privacy Act of 1903, which was passed by the New York state legislature in response to a 1902 court decision.

The plaintiff in that case was a little girl whose picture was used to promote the sale of flour without her consent. The New York Court of Appeals ruled that the girl had no common-law right to prevent use of her image but suggested that lawmakers could create a statutory right to privacy.

Other tobacco-card sets were produced in those years before World War I. The American Tobacco Company also issued the over-size T3 Turkey Red Cabinet Cards, large lithographic color cards that collectors redeemed for coupons distributed in packs of its ciga-rettes. It also issued the T205 set, known as the "Gold Border series" (T206 cards had white borders). High-quality T205 cards are diffi-cult to find, because the gold paint on the borders was prone to chip-ping, which is a shame, because some collectors say that the T205 series is the most beautiful set ever made.

Olbermann is certainly a fan: "The gold borders are distinctive enough but the intricacy of the card designs was just as innovative," he wrote in a T205 history that comes with Topps T205, a tribute to the series issued in 2003. "American League cards didn't look like National League cards and the minor leaguers in the set didn't look like either of them."

Another series that gets raves for design was the T204 set, also known as the "Ramly series." (Ramly was one of the cigarette brands manufactured by the Mentor Company of Boston.) The T204 set fea-tured embossed gold borders and vivid black-and-white portraits and included 121 players, including Hall of Famers Johnson, Plank, Christy Mathewson, Cy Young, Ty Cobb, and Nap Lajoie. The T201 series, found in Mecca cigarettes, featured a nifty innovation: It was the first card that came with player stats. Even better, when the card was folded, a second player appeared, although he shared the legs and shoes of the player displayed when the card was open. Hassan Cigarettes fired back with a triple-folded card that offered a baseball action scene sandwiched between two ballplayer portraits.

Other industries recognized baseball cards as a way to grab the attention of young consumers. The weekly newspapers *Sporting Life* and the *Sporting News* issued card sets. So did candy, cookie, and gum manufacturers. Collectors still go nuts for the cards featuring the scores of players that were offered in boxes of Cracker Jack in 1914 and 1915.

A golden age of baseball cards ended abruptly with America's entry into World War I. Cardboard, paper, and ink—not to mention manpower—were needed for the war effort, and the hobby fell on hard times. The war, of course, ended in 1918, but the Black Sox gambling scandal tainted baseball, and interest in the game and baseball cards further dwindled. Thanks to Babe Ruth and the great New York Yankees teams of the 1920s, baseball bounced back. Cards, however, didn't. The tobacco companies completely dropped out in the twenties, and although a few candy and ice cream manufacturers remained in the game, the Roaring Twenties represented a dry period for baseball cards.

One development in the Jazz Age, however, would revolutionize the world of baseball cards for later generations. In 1928 the Frank H. Fleer Company of Philadelphia refined a formula for chewing gum it had been working on for decades. The first commercially successful bubble gum hit store shelves soon after that, and the Goudey

Gum Company of Boston issued a set that was the very first to come with a piece of bubble gum. More important to modern collectors, the cards in the 1933 Goudey series were made with silkscreen printing that gave them a wide range of vivid colors. Most of the stars of the day—including Babe Ruth, Dizzy Dean, Jimmie Foxx, and Lefty Grove—were represented, and kids went crazy that summer trying to track down their favorite players and complete the series. But there was a rub: Goudey said there were 240 cards in the set but issued only 239. Card 106 was intentionally withheld as a marketing ploy to keep customers coming back for another pack. Goudey finally issued card number 106 the following year, and collectors who complained about the ruse were sent the card, which pictured the retired Napoleon Lajoie. It is now, like the T206 Wagner, rare, expensive, and much desired.

Meanwhile there was a factory worker from Syracuse who had become obsessed with collecting and cataloging trading cards. Jefferson Burdick published *The American Card Catalog* in 1933, the first attempt to create a Dewey decimal system for trading cards. Burdick was widely hailed as the father of trading-card collecting, and even seventy years ago he knew that the Wagner card was something special; *The American Card Catalog* listed the value of most cards at a nickel or a dime, but the Wagner was worth a then-unbelievable $50.

Burdick suffered from arthritis, and the pain was so debilitating that he could not open his mouth wide enough to slip in a ball of candy, much less chew a stick of bubble gum. He was a slight, frail man, a lifelong bachelor considered peculiar by many of his coworkers, and according to his friends he never attended a baseball game in his life. Yet Burdick put together one of the greatest collections in history, systematically organizing trading cards into various categories and designations that are still in use today. The T206 label, for example, tells collectors that a card is a twentieth-century tobacco edition. Candy and gum cards issued after 1930 received an R. (R414-11, for example, refers to the 1957 Topps series.) There wasn't much of a mystery to Burdick's system—he simply took the "T" from "tobacco" and issued a series of numbers after the letter.

"All he was interested in was cards," his friend John DeFlores once told the *Syracuse Post-Standard*. "He was a bachelor and that hobby was his life's work."

In 1947, Burdick traveled to New York's Metropolitan Museum of Art and announced his intention to donate his 306,353 cards—including a T206 Wagner—to the Met. His poor health, however, turned the process of organizing and cataloging those cards into a race against time. He retired from his factory job in 1959 and moved to New York so he could be closer to the museum, and after sixteen years of filing and organizing his cards, he finally finished the job on January 10, 1963. The next day he admitted himself to a hospital. He died two months later.

As in World War I, World War II paper and cardboard shortages curtailed production of baseball cards. The first postwar set was issued in 1948 by Bowman Gum, forty-eight black-and-white cards that weren't particularly attractive or inspiring. Chicago's Leaf Company released a hundred-card color set that year but then dropped out of the market. Bowman, which had signed most big-league players to exclusive contracts, seemed to have the field to itself. But in 1951 the Topps Company of Brooklyn, New York, fired the first salvo in what would become known as the 1950s baseball card war. The gum company issued a fifty-two-card Major League All-Star set that was rather unimpressive and not all that popular with kids. But the next year Topps roared back with an issue that still makes collectors' hearts skip a beat: The 407-card 1952 series blew away the competition. The cards were 50 percent larger than Bowman's cards, and they were the first cards to include players' lifetime stats as well numbers from the previous season. The series also included the first Topps Mickey Mantle card, one of the hobby's most sought-after cards.

Bowman sued Topps, claiming that the newcomer had infringed on its contracts with players. Consumers were the winners, however briefly: Both companies issued spectacular sets in the 1950s before Topps bought out Bowman and monopolized the market for the next twenty-five years.

4

A WHOLE NEW STRATOSPHERE

Jim Copeland paid over 400 percent more than Bill Mastro had paid for the card just a few years earlier—and this time around, nobody threw in dozens of other T206 cards—but he had no regrets.

"I bought it because the card is unique," Copeland said. "I paid $110,000 for it because it is beautiful and because it is the best of its kind."

But a mere five years after he began building one of the best collections in the world, Copeland decided it was time to sell. He had gotten into the card game in the first place because it was something he could share with his son, and the boy had grown up and lost interest in cards. Copeland's heart wasn't in it anymore.

"It was taking up a lot of my time," Copeland said. "It was something I enjoyed, and then it was time to move on."

Copeland decided to sell his entire 873-piece collection in one giant sale through Mastro. Mastro was the sole choice, Copeland said. "I only bought stuff from reputable dealers, and Bill was a very reputable dealer."

Mastro approached Sotheby's, the venerable New York auction house, with the consignment. Sotheby's had resisted jumping into sports collectibles—what its executives considered a downscale market—even though prices for vintage cards and sports memorabilia had boomed in previous years. But a sluggish economy had cooled the market for expensive paintings, so the auction house decided to put aside its snootiness, accept the Copeland collection on consignment, and hire Mastro as a consultant.

Some hobby insiders feared that the auction with the fancy name—the Copeland Collection of Important Baseball Cards and Sports Memorabilia auction—would be a bust. The same struggling economy that drove Sotheby's and other high-end auction houses to sell sports memorabilia could prompt big-money collectors to stay at home, they worried. One of the hobby's biggest collectors, in fact, had already announced that he would sit the auction out: A jealous Barry Halper boycotted the event because Sotheby's had termed the Copeland collection the best in the world.

Rumors were also beginning to circulate around the hobby about the Gretzky T206 Wagner. It had been doctored to boost its value, people whispered. Mastro dismissed the rumors as the rants of envious competitors, and that was good enough for most. About eight hundred of the hobby's wealthiest collectors packed into a large room at Sotheby's New York City offices for the March 1991 auction. Others bid by telephone. People who attended described it as a feeding frenzy. A new breed of collector had gotten into the hobby, and the newcomers seemed willing to spend whatever it took. "It was insanity there. It was the showcase of showcases, the World Series," Al "Mr. Mint" Rosen said.

Collectors bid furiously during the first three hours of the two-day auction. A 1952 Topps Mickey Mantle sold for $49,500, more than triple the pre-auction estimate. A complete T206 set—minus Wagner and two other rare cards—went for $99,000.

Shortly after noon, auctioneer Robert Woolley stepped to the podium and announced Lot 196. It needed no introduction—everybody in the giant hall knew it as the most valuable card in the hobby. "And now," Woolley said, "the Holy Grail."

As described by Pete Williams in the book *Card Sharks*, the atmosphere in the room was electric as Woolley called for the opening bid. When he got $228,000—twice the pre-sale estimate—the crowd gasped, as if the air had been sucked out of the room. The bidding continued in increments of $10,000, with a "secret" bidder joining in by telephone. Mike Gidwitz was prepared to spend $300,000 to secure The Card, and when Woolley got to that magic number, the room broke out in applause. But it was the unidentified bidder on the phone—with Bill Mastro listening in—who was driving the auction. When Gidwitz or Aspen, Colorado, collector Mark Friedland would make a bid, the phone bidder would immediately up the ante. Friedland went past the limit he had set for himself—$330,000—and the bidding continued. The phone bidder pledged $400,000, and the crowd erupted in applause again. Friedland countered with $405,000, but when the phone bidder countered with $410,000, the Coloradan dropped out. Sotheby's 10 percent buyer's premium added $41,000 to the price, bringing the final tab to $451,000, a figure that sent the world of baseball cards into a whole new stratosphere.

The secret bidder, of course, was a novice collector named Wayne Gretzky, who just happened to be the best player in the history of the National Hockey League. Gretzky purchased The Card with his boss, Bruce McNall, the flamboyant owner of the NHL's Los Angeles Kings, who had made a fortune as a coin collector. Coins were a profitable venture, but they didn't generate headlines, and the Southern California native became the toast of Los Angeles when he bought the Kings in 1987 and acquired Gretzky from the Edmonton Oilers the following year.

The two became fast friends as Gretzky turned sunny Los Angeles into a hockey town and McNall perfected the art of living large,
investing in movie studios, rare coins, and racehorses.

Copeland was a big winner that night at Sotheby's, at least as far
as his T206 Wagner was concerned. His collection went for about $5
million, but he'd sold his pristine T206 Wagner for four times what
he paid for it. (It is believed he lost money on the collection overall
as a result of overpaying for many of his items in the first place.) The
hobby also got a boost—it couldn't buy better publicity than it received after a handsome superstar and his freewheeling employer
spent an outrageous sum to buy the hottest baseball card in history.
And perhaps the biggest winner was Bill Mastro, who proved to the
world that a pugnacious card dealer could organize a major auction.
Mastro spent the next four years with Sotheby's, where he met a new
class of high-roller collectors and absorbed all he could about the
auction business.

"Really, that was the first auction of any substance," Mastro said.
"It gave our industry credibility."

THE FLYING DUTCHMAN

The big orange-and-black T206 mural on the redbrick walls of American Legion Post 82 greets motorists as they enter the city limits of Carnegie, Pennsylvania, one of the first things they see as they head down the narrow, tree-lined road toward the old factory town and one of the few reminders of Honus Wagner in his birthplace.

There is a small roadside historical plaque and a residential building for seniors and the disabled called the Honus Wagner Apartments. A football field used by local high schools is named for Wagner. A Carnegie baseball field is named after NFL legend Mike Ditka.

"I guess we got our metaphors crossed," said Marcella McGrogan, the matronly director of the Historical Society of Carnegie.

It is hardly surprising that Wagner's hometown would honor him with a mural of his baseball card. Although Honus looks stiff and not quite real in the picture, like the portraits of saints that hang in old Byzantine churches, it is one of the few reminders baseball fans have of the man widely considered to be the greatest shortstop ever. In fact, Wagner's baseball card seems to have become more significant to twenty-first-century baseball fans than Wagner himself. Without it, Honus might have completely faded into oblivion, a name known only to baseball historians and die-hard Pirates fans. Like fellow Hall of Famers Roger Bresnahan, King Kelly, and Tim Keefe, he might have become one of those superstars of yesteryear that nobody remembers today.

As a player, Wagner is not a household name to today's fans, and it is difficult to imagine that even he would have ever believed that his baseball card would be worth a million dollars.

"My grandfather was not a materialistic man," said granddaughter Leslie Blair, Wagner's only living descendant. "He wouldn't understand why people are making such a fuss over it. He was such a down-to-earth person. I think he would have thought the whole thing insane."

Blair was only five years old when her grandfather—she called him "Buck"—died in late 1955, and some of her memories of him are fuzzy. Some, however, are crystal clear. She would snuggle in his lap as he sat in a big easy chair, chewing tobacco and feeding her broken pieces of a Hershey bar. Strangers would constantly approach him as they walked down the streets of the blue-collar town.

"He never shooed people away," Blair said fifty-one years after his death. "My grandfather was a sweet, gentle, wonderful man."

He was also one hell of a baseball player. With all due respect to Babe Ruth, Joe DiMaggio, and Willie Mays, Honus Wagner may have been the best the game has ever seen. Said baseball writer and statistician Bill James, "There is no one who has ever played this game that I would be more anxious to have on a baseball team."

Honus Wagner was an eight-time National League batting champion who hit over .300 during his first seventeen years in the big leagues and finished his twenty-one-year career with a lifetime average of .329. He was a powerful hitter who held his heavy bat—more than forty ounces—with his hands several inches apart, a grip that allowed him to slap outside pitches to right field or slide his hands together to pull inside pitches down the left-field line. Wagner was a stocky man, so bowlegged that someone once said he couldn't catch a pig in an alley, but he was a speed demon on the base paths, who led the National League in thefts five times and stole 722 lifetime bases, tenth on baseball's list of career stolen bases.

Wagner was just as good defensively. The Flying Dutchman played every position but catcher during his long career (though when backup catcher Harry Smith fell ill during the 1903 season, Pirates player-manager Fred Clarke told Wagner he'd have to suit up if first-string backup Ed Phelps got hurt). Wagner also took the mound for two games, striking out six and holding opponents scoreless in 8.1 innings of relief work. He even filled in as manager when Clarke was unavailable.

Many students of baseball history consider Wagner the greatest shortstop in baseball history, in an era when baseball was a rough, physical game, but he didn't play the position until 1901, his fifth season in the big leagues. Clarke was eager to dump regular short-stop Fred Ely, an injury-plagued .200 hitter who, Clarke learned, was also a spy paid to lure Pittsburgh players to the fledgling American League. Wagner's versatility made him a suitable replacement, but Wagner was not happy with Clarke's move, and he complained loudly. After years of being shuffled between first, third, and the out-field, Wagner had finally found a home in right field and didn't want to move again. Besides, he believed that playing shortstop affected his hitting.

But once Wagner settled in, he became the game's gold standard at short. His speed and big-cat reflexes made him a machine on the left side of the field; because of his magnificent range, he was cred-ited with errors on balls other shortstops never would have reached.

His huge hands gobbled up ground balls. His first basemen often complained about being pelted with dirt and stones; catching a throw from Wagner was like facing a firing squad.

Wagner had a rocket arm that caused Clarke fits; the shortstop was so confident in his ability to make the throw to first that he often took his time, turning routine plays into nail-biters. Wagner's massive hands made one of the tall tales he told at banquets and Carnegie saloons entirely plausible: "It was late in the day and getting dark. The batter hit a ground ball toward me. Just at that time, a rabbit ran onto the field. I grabbed the rabbit and threw it to first instead of the ball. The batter was out by a hare."

It's hard to overstate Wagner's contributions to the game. Baseball was brutal at the turn of the twentieth century, and ballplayers were seen as a disreputable lot that drank, smoked, gambled, and caroused. Jan Finkel, a member of the Society for American Baseball Research who has written extensively about Wagner, said the Flying Dutchman was certainly no prude—he most definitely liked his liquor, liked to smoke and chew tobacco, and wasn't above spiking a second baseman or slamming a base runner with his glove on close plays. Like most players of his era, Wagner probably gambled on baseball—although he has never been accused of throwing games.

But Wagner's friendly, folksy, self-deprecating demeanor was a big hit with fans. He would hang out at the ballpark for hours after a game to chat with them and sign autographs. He played sandlot ball with Carnegie kids, teaching them the fundamentals. To the nation's huge German-American population, he was a symbol of their success, proof they could not only endure in their new country but excel in it. Wagner helped make baseball respectable.

"Wagner," said Finkel, "was beloved."

When the American League declared itself a major league in 1901, it held itself out as a family-friendly alternative to the ruffians in the senior circuit and promptly began raiding NL rosters. The National League initially underestimated the threat, and a nasty roster war left it bruised and bloodied. But it survived, thanks in part to its best and most popular player: Wagner steadfastly refused to entertain offers to jump ship. The Pirates lost few players to the AL-NL battle—among the reasons they were one of the National League's best teams from 1900 to 1909.

Wagner's highest honor came in 1936, when the Baseball Writers Association of America selected him and four other baseball greats—Babe Ruth, Ty Cobb, Christy Mathewson, and Walter Johnson—for the Baseball Hall of Fame's inaugural class. The induction ceremony was held in 1939, after the Cooperstown museum was completed, and by then Wagner was an overweight man who spent much of his time drinking and spinning yarns. But he acted like a boy on that afternoon in front of a huge crowd, playing in an exhibition contest as if it were a World Series game, putting on one last show for the fans.

"When I was a kid, I said, 'I hope someday I'll be playing in this league,'" he told the crowd of fifteen thousand, three times Cooperstown's population. "And by chance I did."

Unlike those of Cooperstown classmates Cobb and Ruth, the memories of Wagner's accomplishments have faded with time. Ruth remains a commanding influence on American culture decades after his death, a name synonymous with awe-inspiring home runs and larger-than-life appetites.

Cobb, Honus Wagner's contemporary and sometime rival, is still remembered as a ferocious and often mean-spirited competitor who would do just about anything—spike opposing players, brawl with fans—to win.

Honus Wagner? There's a statue honoring him outside Pittsburgh's PNC Park, but the rest of baseball nation has largely forgotten him. He has never been the subject of a bestselling book or a hit movie. He has been the subject of two serious biographies, both published in the mid-1990s, forty years after his death. The only film made about Wagner was a made-for-TV flick called *The Winning Season*. It was a baseball fantasy based on a children's book called *Honus and Me*, which was about a boy who finds a magic T206 Wagner in an old lady's attic and is transported back in time to the 1909 World Series. In the movie version, Wagner is portrayed as a bit of a ladies' man, something he most definitely was not in real life.

"They took a beautiful children's story and turned him into a womanizer," the historical society's Wagner expert Carol Dlugos said disapprovingly. "I guess they made it for the slut generation."

Pete Enfield, the vice president of CMG Worldwide, the intellectual-property-rights management company that represents the Wagner estate (i.e., granddaughter Leslie Blair), said that Wagner still resonates with baseball purists but casual fans don't know much about him. The agency has netted some deals for his name and likeness—primarily with trading-card companies and video-game manufacturers—that have generated almost $1 million since 1988. That's a pittance compared to the millions generated by CMG Worldwide's big three: Ruth, Marilyn Monroe, and James Dean. (The latter two can bring up to $7 million a year lending their likenesses and names to products.)

"Deals don't come by easily for Honus," Enfield said.

There are many reasons Wagner has gone AWOL in America's consciousness. Despite its recent renaissance, Pittsburgh's decades-old decline hasn't helped: A dwindling population and economic base mean there are fewer hometown businesses disposed to build marketing campaigns around Honus. Timing, too, is everything. Wagner's awesome talent was never captured by mass media. His career ended while radio and film were in their infancy and television was still a futuristic fantasy. And although Wagner was one of the great hitters of his time, he played in the dead-ball era and finished his career with just 101 home runs—a stat that hardly inspires awe in this steroid-bloated era.

But Pete Enfield believes that the most significant reason is Wagner's personality. Wagner, unfortunately for his legacy, didn't have larger-than-life appetites like Ruth. He wasn't a violent man like Cobb. He didn't marry a glamorous move star, like Joe DiMaggio.

Honus Wagner was a nice, normal guy, the kind of man who blends in easily in a small town like Carnegie.

"He enjoyed being a father and a husband," Leslie Blair said. "He didn't really care about popularity."

This may be the primary reason that the only thing keeping Honus Wagner's memory from slipping away is his baseball card. The very same personality traits that made Wagner a good husband, father, and neighbor make him easy to overlook. And that's a shame. Honus Wagner deserves better than to fade away with the dusty ghosts of another time.

"He wasn't just the greatest shortstop ever," teammate Tommy Leach once said. "He was the greatest everything ever."

John Peter Wagner—Honus is a diminutive of Johan, or John in German—was born on February 24, 1874 in Chartiers, Pennsylvania, twenty years before that small community consolidated with neighboring Mansfield to create a new municipality called Carnegie, after western Pennsylvania's most prominent citizen. Andrew Carnegie was the embodiment of the American dream, an impoverished but self-educated Scottish immigrant who became one of the wealth-iest men in America. Carnegie's hard work and vision turned U.S. Steel into one of the most powerful corporations in the world and helped make the United States into an economic power, and the residents of this newly minted town hoped that some of his good fortune would rub off on them.

They were right: In 1901, the union-busting industrialist–turned–philanthropist endowed the town with the Andrew Carnegie Free Library and Music Hall, the imposing Italianate cultural center that sits on a hill in the center of town, surrounded by broad lawns and big, wide trees. (Carnegie's generosity didn't stop in Pennsylvania. He gave away more than $350 million before his death in 1919 to fund the establishment of schools, libraries, and universities.)

Honus was one of nine children, three of whom died in infancy, born to Peter and Katheryn Wagner, immigrants from Prussia who settled in a rough, working-class neighborhood shortly after they arrived in the United States in 1866. Peter and Katheryn preferred to speak German at home, but their kids were bilingual and spoke English with western Pennsylvania accents. The Wagners' five boys had all-American tastes when it came to play: Baseball was their favorite game. Wagner attended school for six years, but secondary education was not available in western Pennsylvania until the 1890s, so at the age of twelve he joined his father and three older brothers in the coal mines. He later found work in a steel mill and helped out at his brother Charley's barbershop. Evenings and Sun-days were for baseball. Al Wagner, two and a half years older than Honus and the best player in Carnegie, convinced his friends to let his little brother play when they needed an extra. He told his brother to learn every position. That way he would always have a spot on the team.

The Wagner brothers picked up a few dollars plus winnings from side bets playing for community teams and clubs sponsored by churches and businesses, but in 1895, Al became a real professional when he signed a contract with the Steubenville, Ohio, franchise of the Inter-State League. Al convinced Steubenville owner George Moreland to sign Honus as a pitcher and a utility fielder. Wagner's first professional contract paid him $35 a month. The Steubenville team folded before the season's end, and Honus eventually embarked on what turned out to be a whirlwind minor-league journey, playing for five teams in three leagues and three states over five months. He played every position but catcher that season, refining his skills, sharpening his game against increasingly difficult competition.

Honus Wagner was a talented but still-raw player in the winter of 1896, when Ed Barrow came to Carnegie to talk to the Wagner brothers about playing for his Wheeling, West Virginia, team. Barrow was already impressed with Al, but he wasn't sure about the awkward-looking younger Wagner, even though he'd been intrigued by the twenty-one-year-old Honus's strength and speed the previous summer when he'd seen him play against Wheeling in the Iron and Oil League. Barrow found Wagner and some pals engaged in a "throwing match" at the Carnegie railroad yard. Wagner didn't look like much of a ballplayer, with his long arms, bowed legs, and a goofy derby sporting a chicken feather in the band, but Barrow's doubts quickly evaporated.

"While I was coming toward them, he turned and fired that big heavy rock a good three hundred feet," Barrow later told the *New York Times*'s Red Smith. "I signed him then and there for $125 a month."

It was a lot of money at the time—the average worker only earned $439 a year in 1896—but it was one of the best decisions Barrow ever made. And this was a man who made a lot of good decisions: Barrow became the Red Sox manager who converted Babe Ruth from pitcher to outfielder, and later served as the chief executive of the New York Yankees, winning fourteen pennants and ten World Series between 1921 and 1945. Among the accomplishments listed on Barrow's plaque in Cooperstown: "Discovered Honus Wagner."

Barrow bought an interest in a minor-league team in Paterson, New Jersey, and Wagner went east to play ball, immediately justifying Barrow's faith in him. He drew attention from National League scouts, too, playing everywhere he was needed and hitting .313 in his first season in Paterson. Executives who came to Paterson to see him play were turned off by his physical appearance, much as some were by Seabiscuit, the funny-looking Thoroughbred that would beat War Admiral in a match race and go on to become an American hero. Boston manager Frank Selee said he would not pay a dime for Wagner, and Phillies manager George Stallings said he couldn't justify paying Wagner's train fare to Philadelphia.

Louisville Colonels owner Barney Dreyfuss and his player-manager Clarke were equally unimpressed. But Louisville club secretary Harry Pulliam saw something special in the barrel-chested, muscular Wagner and convinced his colleagues to take a chance. Wagner debuted with Louisville in July 1897 and hit .338 in sixty-one games. He quickly established himself as a fan favorite, thanks to his easy smile and his gentle way.

Persistent financial problems convinced National League officials to downsize from twelve to eight teams, and Louisville, baseball's smallest and southernmost market, was one of the four clubs dissolved. Dreyfuss bought a share of the Pirates and became the team president. He brought his most accomplished players, including Wagner, north with him. In the decade that followed, Wagner was the best player on one of baseball's best teams. The Pirates won the

National League pennant in 1901, 1902, and 1903, thanks to Wagner's contributions.

Dreyfuss challenged the fledgling American League to a best-of-nine championship series in 1903, and the Boston Pilgrims—they later became the Red Sox—beat Pittsburgh five games to three in what was a humiliating experience for Wagner: He committed six errors and went 1-for-14 in the last four games. To make things worse, he made the final out of the series on a called strike. Sportswriters implied that Wagner was "yellow." It was a slight that would haunt him for years.

His greatest season came in 1908, when he hit .354 to easily lead the league in batting average (players in both the American League and the National League averaged .239 that year). He was tops in just about every other category, too, that season. Lee Sinin's *Sabermetric Baseball Encyclopedia* said it added up to a .878 OBS (on-base percentage plus slugging percentage, a term that entered the baseball lexicon about ten years ago), the greatest offensive season in NL history until Barry Bonds shattered the single-season home-run record in 2001. Still, the Pirates fell short that season. They could have forced a three-way tie for the National League pennant with the Chicago Cubs and New York Giants by beating the Cubs in the last game of the season, but they lost—thanks in part to Wagner's two errors—and fans and the press once again talked about how the Pirates choked when the pressure was on.

The 1909 season—the year the American Tobacco Company began production of its T206 series—would be different. It was the year Dreyfuss opened Forbes Field, one of the first-generation steel-and-concrete stadiums that replaced nineteenth-century wooden ballparks. The Pirates immediately took to their new home—they won 110 games that year in a 153-game season (one game with St. Louis was rained out and not rescheduled), with Wagner again among the National League leaders in offensive categories. In one of his more notable appearances, he stole his way around the bases in the first inning of a May 2 nightcap against the Chicago Cubs, setting an NL record as the first player ever to pull off the feat three times. Amazingly, he would duplicate the effort again the following day.

The Pirates went back to the World Series once more, this time against Ty Cobb, the American League's best player, and the Detroit Tigers. The Pirates won in seven games, thanks to Wagner's outstanding play. He hit .333, compared to Cobb's .231. He drove in six runs and stole six bases—a World Series record that would last until Lou Brock stole seven for the Cardinals in 1967. Nobody was calling Wagner "yellow" any longer.

The following season was a disappointing one for Wagner. The Pirates were never in contention and finished in third place behind New York and Chicago. Wagner hit .320, but that was only due to a late-season surge. Like many players of the era, he enjoyed a drink, and by 1910 his drinking escalated, and he slumped most of the season. He got into uncharacteristically ugly confrontations with teammates, opponents, and umpires. And then the American Tobacco Company issued the card that he hated.

Wagner had big seasons in 1911 and 1912 before his career started its slow decline, hitting exactly .300 in 1913, the last time he would hit or pass that mark. The Pirates, too, began to skid. The team finished seventh in 1914, fifth in 1915, sixth in '16. Barney Dreyfuss asked Wagner to become the Pirates' player-manager in 1917, but he quit as skipper after the first four games of the season. He played his last game on September 17, 1917—three innings at second base. Wagner left the game holding several major-league records: games, at-bats, hits, extra-base hits, runs, and total bases. He held the National League record for doubles, triples, and batting titles. His 1,732 RBI were second only to Cap Anson's 1,870.

Wagner's legacy, however, went beyond the numbers. His easygoing nature had made the game respectable for the middle class. He was an immigrant's kid who used baseball to lift himself out of poverty; he embodied the American dream for the millions of newcomers who were pouring into Ellis Island.

6

CITIZEN WAGNER

Honus Wagner, abiding bachelor, finally settled down after the 1916 season, marrying his longtime girlfriend, Bessie Smith. Their occasional arguments were sparked by the tobacco juice Wagner sprayed on the floor when he missed the living room spittoon. Their first child, Elva, was stillborn in 1918, but Betty was born in 1919, and Virginia arrived in 1922, and Wagner was a loving and conscientious father who doted on his two girls. He called them "my boys" and taught them how to throw, catch, and hit a baseball. Betty married a man named Harry Blair in 1948, and two years later they presented Wagner with his only grandchild, Leslie. Wagner worshipped the little girl he called "Honey."

"In the last days of his life, he was semiconscious," Blair said. "I was the only one he recognized."

America had entered World War I in April 1917, and after Wagner retired, he threw himself into the war effort against Germany, his parents' native land. Wagner had never been comfortable as a public speaker during the early years of his career, but he put aside his nerves and made numerous speeches urging Americans to buy Liberty Bonds. In fact, he spent much of his life after baseball on the lecture circuit, giving talks to fraternal organizations and business groups. He was appointed to several political positions—he was named the Pennsylvania State fish commissioner and the sergeant-at-arms of the Pennsylvania legislature—and he coached numerous sports teams, including the Carnegie High football team and the Carnegie Institute of Technology (now Carnegie Mellon) baseball and basketball squads.

He had already planted the seeds for his postbaseball life during his career, and the investments he made with Barney Dreyfuss's help had long ago begun to pay off. Wagner was something of a real estate developer, buying run-down car-repair properties, fixing them up, and renting them out. He had opened one of the first garages in Carnegie—"automobiling" was one of his hobbies. After his retirement he opened a sporting-goods store in Pittsburgh with Pie Traynor, the Hall of Famer who played third base for the Pirates from 1920 to 1937. But the business crashed during the Great Depression, and, like millions of other Americans, Wagner found himself in dire financial straits.

The Pirates offered him a coaching job in 1933, and he eagerly accepted. He turned Arky Vaughan into a Hall of Fame shortstop and worked closely with young players. His primary job, however, seemed to be telling stories to fans and to the Pirates players and coaches. He told the same stories to the kids in the empty lot next to his home. "He'd say, 'Boys, gather 'round, let me tell you all about how I hit a home run all the way to California," Blair said with a giggle, still relishing those silly stories. "'I hit a home run out of Forbes Field, and it landed in a passing coal car. It went straight to California. How about that?' All these little kids would be standing on our porch going, 'Wow.'"

In his later years, Wagner mostly loafed around the shops and joints of Carnegie. He spent a lot of time drinking beer in the down-town Elks Club and the other neighborhood bars, and by the 1940s and '50s many people didn't know about his storied baseball career, much less that he was among the best ever to play the game. To them Wagner was one of Carnegie's boozy old men. He'd walk into a sa-loon and tap a coin on the bar to announce his presence. Those who did know who he was wanted to buy the great Honus Wagner a drink, and he was happy to oblige. But even those beer marathons didn't dull the affection Wagner felt for kids.

"He'd come out of the Elks Club with bottles of Coca-Cola and bags of potato chips for the kids," said Bob Davidson, a Carnegie na-tive who mowed the elderly Wagner's lawn.

When Wagner died at home in 1955, there was a burst of appre-ciation for him. The local newspapers ran stories about his Hall of Fame baseball career, about his tireless support of Carnegie's busi-ness community, about his gentle disposition with local kids. And then the town that Honus Wagner helped build forgot all about him. Wagner was Carnegie's favorite son during his seventeen-year major-league baseball career. He'd become so popular, in fact, that he overshadowed his hometown's namesake, to a point where Andrew Carnegie once threatened to cut off millions of philanthropy dollars to western Pennsylvania during a brief tantrum sparked by his jealousy. The great sportswriter Grantland Rice even memorialized Carnegie's outburst in verse:

Oh, Andy, Andy, Andy—though you stand upon the street
And shovel out a million onto every guy you meet; though you blow
*   a half a billion, you will never have the call*
As the greatest man in Pittsburg while H. Wagner hits the ball

In the years after Wagner's retirement in 1917, though, the long shadow he cast on his hometown waned.

Carnegie, Pennsylvania, was a vibrant immigrant community in Honus Wagner's day, a smorgasbord of ethnic groups—German, Irish, Italian, Polish, Ukrainian, Russian, and more—that traded political oppression, religious persecution, and economic deprivation for the promise of American freedom and prosperity. The town had a bustling business center, and people from outlying farms and mining camps would ride trains into town to shop, worship, and socialize in Carnegie's saloons, theaters, churches, and shops. Signs of those good times are still scattered throughout Wagner's hometown, the place where he spent the vast majority of his life. The Andrew Carnegie Free Library and Music Hall is still the heart of the community.

Carnegie's residential neighborhoods are lined with sturdy turn-of-the-century homes; the surrounding hills are rugged reminders of Carnegie's long history as a coal town. Many immigrants found work in the nearby mines, including Honus Wagner's father Peter (Wagner's "Flying Dutchman" nickname was a misnomer). When he was old enough, Honus found work in the mines, too, at least briefly.

Mining towns ride boom-and-bust cycles, but modern-day Carnegie looks like it's been busted for a long, long time. Main Street is lined with empty storefronts and businesses that have seen better days. For Rent and For Sale signs sprout up on front lawns all over town. The community's population in 2000, according to the U.S. Census, was 8,389, about a third less than the 12,663 counted in 1940. A giant mural on a downtown wall features a phoenix rising from the ashes, but optimism is hard to find in Carnegie.

"I don't like this town anymore," said Jim Cancilla, a graying popular-culture maven who owns D&J Records, a music and collectibles store in downtown Carnegie. "I'm getting ready to move to Florida. I sit in this store all day, and maybe one or two people come in. If it weren't for the stuff I sell on eBay, I'd be in trouble."

The collapse of coal, steel, and other Rust Belt industries put a big hurt on western Pennsylvania. (Pittsburgh, the nation's twelfth-largest city in 1950, with 677,000 residents, now ranks fifty-fourth, with a population of 328,000.) Carnegie seems especially jinxed. In September 2004, Hurricane Ivan's heavy rains caused a massive flood—the kind that comes once every five hundred years—damaging hundreds of homes and businesses. Then in October 2005, a fire that originated in a restaurant called the Red Onion scorched Carnegie's small downtown, a shopping district still struggling with the scars left by the flood. The blaze gutted the Red Onion and a neighboring bank; a second bank received massive smoke and water damage. So did the building that housed the Historical Society of Carnegie, home to a significant Honus Wagner memorabilia collection. Months later the burned and crumbling buildings had yet to be torn down or repaired.

"It's a blue-collar town," said Stan Klos, a local entrepreneur, "and it's dying."

Wagner might not even recognize the place. Granddaughter Blair sold her Wagner memorabilia at a 2003 auction for $180,000 and moved to South Carolina. Honus's place of worship, the First Evangelical Lutheran St. John's Church, is now a warehouse for a construction company. His longtime home at 119 Railroad Avenue—Wagner lived there until he married Bessie Smith at age forty-two—is decorated with Pittsburgh Steelers banners and occupied by a family that cares little about baseball history or Wagner.

"The Realtor told me Honus Wagner lived here," said Ryan Schall, the current owner. "But I didn't really know who he was."

After years of neglect, Carnegie's political and business leaders decided to revive the memory of Honus Wagner and turn him into a cornerstone of economic development. Jeff Stephan, the executive director of the Carnegie Community Development Corporation, was the first to suggest a permanent tourist attraction, a museum dedicated to Wagner. Mayor Jim Pascoe and other town leaders hoped to have the museum up and running in time for Major League Baseball's 2006 All-Star Game, scheduled to be held just five miles away at Pittsburgh's PNC Park. Carnegie leaders planned on the first-ever "Wagner Day." Local baseball teams would hold exhibition games, and auto dealers would donate vans to carry out-of-state visitors on tours of Wagner's favorite hangouts. Church groups would sell refreshments. Baseball fans in town for the All-Star Game would spend money in Carnegie businesses.

A temporary Wagner exhibit opened at Carnegie's municipal building in the summer of 2005 while a room at the historical society was being renovated for the Wagner museum. The devastating downtown fire changed everything. McGrogan, a petite grandmother with a fiery passion for hometown history, said the historical society lost some of its files and boxes to Carnegie's twin disasters, but it did save much of its Wagner memorabilia and put it on display at the society's temporary headquarters—the storefront it shared with a thrift store that sells secondhand knickknacks, used books, and other yard-sale castoffs. A glass case was filled with Wagner pictures and memorabilia, including a reprint of the T206 Wagner. A 1907 town directory lists Wagner's occupation as "short stop." A Norman Rockwell–esque painting that was printed on calendars depicts an elderly Honus in his Pirates uniform leaning over to talk to a small boy. (The model was a local kid, Gerry Sgro, one of Wagner's neighborhood favorites.) A book compiled by Dlugos contains locals' memories of the Hall of Famer: Pauline Wagner, who identified herself as a second cousin, reported that her father said Honus would never amount to anything because all he wanted to do was play baseball. Lois O'Donnell remembered how Big Boy, Wagner's massive Great Dane, would walk into Murphy's 5&10, pick a fresh rubber ball out of a display bin, then drop the ball and catch it on a bounce, hoping to get a clerk or customer to play with him. Wagner, O'Donnell added, kept a tab at the store for Big Boy.

The other large stash of Wagner memorabilia in Carnegie belongs to Jim Cancilla, the record-store owner. Wagner's old Railroad Avenue home was renovated about twenty years ago, and decades' worth of Wagner-family personal items were dragged to the curb. Cancilla went through the trash and took some of the garbage home. "I'm not a baseball person," he said. "But this stuff was just out there, and I happened to be there." Cancilla refused to talk about his Wagner collection—he's afraid Blair might want the stuff back and cause him problems. "I don't need the attention," he said, refusing to elaborate further. But he later warmed up and pointed to a shelf holding seventies lunch boxes, *Gunsmoke* toys, and an old Super 8 movie camera. "See that camera?" he asked. "That was his. They don't make things like that anymore."

The historical society was out of commission indefinitely, but a group of entrepreneurs led by Stanley Klos stepped up for the Flying Dutchman. The group behind Warner Carnegie Incorporated bought the three-story Beechwood Avenue home Honus had built after he married Bessie and announced their intention to turn it into a bed-and-breakfast and Wagner museum. Wagner, who lived in the home until his death, took an active role in the house's design and construction, and although the home had been split into two apartments, it still retained many of its original fixtures and furnishings. Klos bought the house for $130,000 and acquired Wagner's original plans and other building documents for the house at a December 2005 auction.

"With the original plans, we know exactly what went in that house in 1918 and what didn't," he says. "We could re-create his original plan."

Honus Wagner's hometown could barely contain its apathy. The borough's zoning board twice turned down requests for a variance that would have allowed the project to proceed, because neighbors expressed concerns about parking. The entrepreneurs tried to auction off the house on eBay, but while the listing got thousands of hits, it received no bids. Klos and his group finally decided to list the house with a local Realtor.

"This has been frustrating," said Klos's partner, Michael Gissin. "Maybe with renewed attention we can get Carnegie to reconsider, if not for us, then for the new owners. But right now we've had enough."

In a nation where deep-pocketed collectors eagerly paid more than $1 million for a baseball card, the pale brick house looked like a good deal: For a mere $199,900, a baseball fan could pick up a three-story home built by a Hall of Famer, complete with four bedrooms, hardwood floors, stained-glass windows, gas fireplaces, and a big front porch. Klos's son Louis, a Virginia Tech student, spent the summer of 2006 helping to clean up the house.

"I've looked under every floorboard I can," he said. "This would be a great summer if I found a T206 Wagner."

7

HONUS GETS A MAKEOVER

Wayne Gretzky gave the T206 Wagner that now bears his name a splash of celebrity, a shot of glamour that was surely missing in a hobby that had begun to be dominated by obsessive men that outsiders, even those who collected baseball cards themselves, viewed as strange, vaguely dangerous . . . not far from the image of Terence Stamp chloroforming Samantha Eggar in his basement in the eerie classic *The Collector.*

Gretzky is the antithesis of that creepy image—the Great One is the most accomplished player in NHL history, a superstar who brought hockey to new peaks of popularity and electrified arenas from Vancouver to Miami. Gretzky-led teams won four Stanley Cups, and he holds or shares sixty-one NHL records, including most goals in a season (92), most assists in a season (163), and most points in a season (215). He also notched more goals (894), assists (1,963), and points (2,857) than any other player in NHL history.

Gretzky wasn't just a boldfaced name on the ice. His life had become gossip-page fodder in 1988 when he married actress Janet Jones, the blond bombshell from *The Flamingo Kid* and other films. In 2006 the couple's star power was dulled after prosecutors linked Jones to a New Jersey–based gambling ring allegedly run by Gretzky's former teammate, Rick Tocchet (prosecutors said Jones had placed at least $100,000 in bets with bookies). But in 1991 the only athlete who could match Wayne Gretzky's global fame was Chicago Bulls great Michael Jordan.

Gretzky, however, wasn't much of a baseball-card collector. The T206 Wagner didn't give him goose bumps or chills, didn't fill a hole in his soul or lend him a spiritual connection to a long-gone time or hero—some of the emotions that fuel the serious collectors' purchases. For Rob Lifson, before it became a business, collecting baseball cards was the way to follow the story line in a very-long-running drama. For others it's a way to make order out of chaos, a way to gain control of an out-of-control world. For Gretzky it was simply something he bought for a lot of money and hoped to sell for even more.

"For me it was an investment," Gretzky said. "At the time all these memorabilia things were increasing in value. It was an outrageous amount of money, but we thought the market would remain strong.

"Still . . . my dad told me I was an idiot for paying $450,000 for a baseball card."

The brains behind the deal belonged to Bruce McNall, a savvy businessman who also owned Gretzky's hockey team, the Los Angeles Kings. McNall has been called a lot of things—con man, hustler, federal inmate—but when it came to money, nobody ever called McNall an idiot.

"My philosophy was, if you buy something that is absolutely the best in the world, you'd be okay because there is always another buyer for something at the top end," McNall said during a 2005 interview. "This thing keeps going up in value, and it will end up being who knows how much."

Like the card he purchased with Wayne Gretzky, McNall's wealth and fame was built more on hype than substance. The foundation of

McNall's business empire was tall tales, borrowed money, and supersized chutzpah, and a few years after he bought the card, it all came tumbling down—McNall would plead guilty to defrauding banks of $236 million and was sentenced to seventy months in a federal prison. He was shackled chain-gang style for a while and moved to prisons all around the country—from Safford, Arizona, to Oklahoma City to Milan, Michigan. He was released in 2001, but his probation didn't ended until 2006.

But during the 1980s and early '90s, when McNall owned the Kings and relaxed in his private box at the Great Western Forum with Michelle Pfeiffer, Tom Hanks, Goldie Hawn, Kurt Russell, and Sylvester Stallone, he liked to tell people that he was worth hundreds of millions of dollars. He bragged that he'd raked in $1,000 a week trading coins as a kid while most of his peers were mowing lawns and delivering newspapers—not terribly unlike the young Lifson and Mastro. He said he attended Oxford and had done business with J. Paul Getty and Howard Hughes.

They were great stories that made for compelling profiles in sports magazines and newspaper sports sections—problem was, none of it was true. "Those legends just get greater and greater," McNall sighed when confronted by *Forbes* magazine in 1991 about the fibs in his résumé. "They're just not correct."

It's easy to see how McNall sold his wares: His charm is difficult to resist. He's a stout man with a warm personality and a ready laugh—his pal and business partner, the comedian John Candy, who died in 1994, would have been perfect in the lead role of *The Bruce McNall Story*. He always had time and a clever quip for reporters, always had a way of making people feel comfortable—a light touch on the shoulder, a soft chuckle. He was eager to please Kings fans, eager to bring the Stanley Cup to Los Angeles. He spent a fortune on high-salaried players like Paul Coffey and Jari Kurri. He gave lavish gifts to employees and friends. He threw extravagant parties for his players. While most teams flew commercial, the Kings were one of the first teams to travel in their own team jet.

"When you talk to him," Gretzky wrote in his autobiography, "it's like talking to your favorite uncle."

McNall grew up in Arcadia, California, a bright but heavyset kid who must have felt out of place growing up among the beautiful people of Southern California. McNall later said that his problems stemmed from his need for acceptance, a hunger for applause and attention. He certainly wasn't much of an athlete, although he was a champion at Monopoly. "He always went for the high-priced stuff like Boardwalk and Park Place," his mother, Shirley, once said. "And he would always beat us. His basic philosophy even then was that you had to spend money to make money."

Like many men who grew up in the 1950s and '60s, McNall was into baseball cards, and he also collected stamps. But his real passion was coins. He began collecting coins when he was eight years old, and he was so obsessed he would get his mother to drive him to local banks, where he would ask to inspect coin rolls, hoping to find rare pennies. McNall received a bachelor's degree from UCLA in three years and planned to pursue his doctorate in ancient history.

"I was always fascinated with history," McNall said. "Basically, I've always been a history buff, and my main area was ancient Roman coins."

But he realized he could make far more money in the coin business than he ever would as a professor, so he dropped out of school and opened a coin shop called Numismatic Fine Arts in Beverly Hills. McNall soon became one of the most prominent dealers in the world, although he later confessed to a celebrity-profile writer from

Vanity Fair that his coin profits came primarily from smuggling old coins past customs agents.

McNall used his wealth to branch out into entertainment and sports. He produced several movies, including *The Fabulous Baker Boys, Mr. Mom,* and *WarGames,* and by all appearances he was a successful Hollywood tycoon. He owned nine cars, including a Bentley, a gold Mercedes, and a Rolls-Royce. He had a private jet to fly him to his seven homes, including his mansion in Hawaii.

McNall was just as eager to make a name for himself in the world of sports. His first foray was the NBA; he purchased a minority interest in the Dallas Mavericks in 1976 but sold it three years later. In 1986 he purchased an interest in the Los Angeles Kings from fellow coin buff Jerry Buss, the owner of the Los Angeles Lakers. Two years later he bought Buss out and became the Kings' sole owner.

McNall understood that the Kings, perpetual NHL doormats, needed star power, something to turn sunny Southern California into a hockey haven, and he helped engineer a deal that brought Gretzky from the Edmonton Oilers to Los Angeles. While Gretzky was turning the Kings into contenders, McNall was perfecting the art of living large. His colt Saumarez won the Prix de l'Arc de Triomphe, France's most prestigious race, in 1990. Along with John Candy, McNall and Gretzky purchased the Toronto Argonauts of the Canadian Football League. McNall enticed Notre Dame star Raghib "Rocket" Ismail away from the NFL by signing him to a four-year deal for a then-unheard-of $18.2 million contract. Led by Ismail, the Argos won the CFL's 1991 Grey Cup championship

McNall also formed a partnership with Upper Deck, the trading-card manufacturer, to create Upper Deck Authenticated, a company that would sign exclusive contracts with big-name stars such as Gretzky and Joe Montana to sell autographed sports collectibles.

He decided to buy what would become known as the Gretzky T206 Wagner on a whim after receiving the Sotheby's catalog for the Copeland auction in the mail. Purchasing The Card with Gretzky, he thought, would be a good way to stir up publicity for Upper Deck Authenticated.

"I called Wayne, I said, 'Hey, Wayne, do you know anything about baseball cards?' I said, 'Let's buy it together, for fun.' The card was appraised at $200,000 at the time. I said, 'Wayne, maybe we can get it for like $250,000.'"

The auction was held just a few days later, with Gretzky and McNall bidding secretly on the phone through Mastro, who was at Sotheby's in New York, even as collectors like Mike Gidwitz tried to keep up. "It blew by $250,000 in a blink," McNall remembered. "I said, 'Wayne, what do you want to do? You want to keep going? Okay, let's go.' And $451,000 was the ultimate price. Afterward, we said, 'Oh, my God, what have we done? Are we nuts?' It was very spontaneous."

The price tag wasn't the only reason McNall and Gretzky developed a bad case of buyer's remorse. Those rumors that the Gretzky T206 Wagner had been altered and restored were churning through the hobby at gale force.

"People were saying it was trimmed. It was a little scary," McNall said. "It was a little disheartening thinking, 'Did we do something stupid?'"

Alan Ray was a hockey fan and a Wayne Gretzky fan, and when he learned that McNall and his star player had spent an eye-popping $451,000 to purchase the card he'd sold to Bill Mastro just a few years earlier for $25,000, he felt as if he'd just lost the Stanley Cup in a one-sided shoot-out. "I liked Gretzky," he said. "I felt bad that he had paid top dollar for that card."

Thanks to the media coverage of the Copeland auction, Ray learned he'd been taken by Mastro that Sunday at Bob Sevchuk's card shop. Mastro spent much of the half hour or so they'd been together bad-mouthing the card, Ray remembered, pointing out its flaws and uneven edges. Of course, Mastro had then spent the years that followed turning it into the most valuable card in the world.

"I had been told by Bill Mastro that the card had not been cut right, but he'll take it off my hands anyway. I had financial problems then, so I had to let it go," Ray said. "Since then people have made a substantial amount of money off this card, and it's not because of the card itself, it's because of how they promoted it."

Of course, Alan Ray had another reason for his bitterness: He knew the real story behind The Card.

At Bob Sevchuk's shop in the dingy Hicksville strip mall in 1985, Ray and Sevchuk committed either the most heinous crime in card-doctoring history or a stunt worthy of the Keystone Kops. The stories they told other hobby veterans about what they did to the Gretzky T206 Honus Wagner PSA 8 NM-MT explains why they've been so hush-hush about the origins of The Card. They also explain why Mastro gets defensive when he's questioned about where exactly The Card came from.

In the early days of the hobby, collectors didn't place tremendous importance on the condition of a card or whether it had been cut from a sheet long after it left the print shop. "Nobody cared about such things," legendary collector Heitman said. "We cut cards out of sheets all the time. Nobody ever paid any attention to things like that."

But as the value of cards skyrocketed in the 1980s, collectors decided they wanted their cards to look like Lauren Bacall or Catherine Deneuve—to withstand the test of time and still look beautiful. Early baseball cards were throwaway items, with no intrinsic value when they were originally manufactured and distributed; vintage cards are valuable because they beat overwhelming odds just to survive.

Cards cut from a sheet decades after the sheet was printed didn't face the same dangers—bicycle spokes, grubby-handed kids, spring cleanings, swampy basements—that cards that came from a pack of cigarettes or gum overcame. Cards that have been altered and restored have been artificially enhanced, like the athletes who use steroids to get an advantage on their rivals. By the time Professional Sports Authenticator and other grading services were established in the 1990s, most collectors looked at cards cut from sheets outside the factory as tainted. PSA and most grading services say they will not grade cards that have been cut from a printer's sheet or restored or enhanced.

The story goes like this: Sevchuk told Zimmerman that Ray's father had purchased an uncut T206 sheet at a flea market in Florida, probably sometime in the early 1980s. Ray's father then sent the sheet to his son to sell in the New York City area. "The number I heard was, they bought it for something like $12 or $112, something like that. The price was relatively modest," said Evan Marx, the owner of a Long Island sports-memorabilia store called BookMarx Collectibles, who said Sevchuk told him the same story. "I believe they cut it right at Sevchuk's store. Yeah, I think they cut it right there."

The T206 sheet would have been an explosive find even then—an uncut sheet would have rocked the vintage-card world like an asteroid slamming into Siberia. It would have been like finding the Dead Sea Scrolls or the Rosetta Stone; no uncut T206 sheets are known to exist. In fact, hobby veterans say no one really knows what an uncut T206 sheet *looks* like.

But this much is certain—it would be worth more than an individual card cut from it. Collectors speculate that an uncut sheet in superior condition featuring Wagner and Plank might fetch $2 million or more. No one knows for sure, of course, since none have ever been offered at auction. The hobby's only uncut T206 proof strip sold for a mere $78,665 at a Mastro Auctions sale in 2002, but that proof strip is badly creased and wrinkled, and its condition is so shabby that it is simply beyond the pale for most collectors. Still, the five-card strip, which features a T206 Wagner, Cy Young, and "Three-Finger" Brown, has great provenance: It was found in the attic of Wagner's home in Carnegie, folded in the back pocket of his uniform pants. Mastro's catalog speculated that the American Tobacco Company might have sent the strip as a last-ditch effort to convince him to sign on with the T206 set, but nobody really knows how Wagner obtained it.

When Sevchuk and Ray decided to slice up that T206 sheet at the Hicksville collectibles store, they not only chopped up a piece of cardboard that might now be even more valuable than the Gretzky T206 Wagner, they destroyed a one-of-a-kind piece of baseball history, an item that would have helped future generations of collectors and historians understand how the T206 series was manufactured and distributed. It's a good thing that Sevchuk and Ray aren't barbers or surgeons: Their technique with scissors or razor blades or whatever they used to slice up that sheet was rank amateur. The cards were horribly cut, and Sevchuk later said they were not uniform in size or shape, but fit together like pieces of a jigsaw puzzle. The Wagner had a red printer's line at the top of the card.

"Some cards were bigger than others," Sevchuk said years later, denying he did the actual surgery. "To my eye the Wagner was not cut right. That's just my opinion."

Lifson agreed that the card wasn't cut properly. Sevchuk had told them at the Hicksville shop that it had come from a sheet. He remembered calling Sevchuk later from his parents' house to ask if there were more sheets where this one had come from—Sevchuk had said in the store that day there might be. "It had an odd shape," Lifson said of The Card. "It was obvious that card had never been in a pack of cigarettes. I've always been adamant about that. They said 'it was in a sheet.' Otherwise, cards don't survive like that."

By the time McNall and Gretzky bought The Card, Alan Ray was livid that Mastro had bullied him into selling it and about the deception that was surrounding it.

And he had proof.

He had photographed the T206 Wagner before he sold it to Mastro, and the card in his photos looked substantially different from the photos he'd seen of McNall and Gretzky's latest acquisition. He sent them to Sotheby's and to Superior Galleries, the Beverly Hills coin-auction house owned at that time by McNall. Sotheby's officials and McNall never responded.

"I didn't even ask for a free hockey ticket," Ray remembered. "But McNall didn't want any part of me. I never heard back from him."

Ray never showed those photographs to reporters who had inquired about The Card. He wanted to hold on to the photographs for the book he planned to write about Mastro and the Gretzky T206 Wagner. "That photo is crucial to the history of The Card, and it is privy to me and to me only," Ray said. "I have to look after mine and my house."

Ray did get a letter a Superior Galleries executive sent after McNall's staff returned the photo of the The Card. Sotheby's officials claim they do not recall the letter or the photograph. Neither does McNall, who now lives near Los Angeles.

"It doesn't mean I didn't get them," McNall said. "But as big a deal as The Card was, in some ways it wasn't that big of a deal. I didn't focus on it. I owned the Kings, the Argonauts, and a film company at the time. I had other things to focus on."

Ray distributed photocopies of the pre-altered card, and at least three still remain in the hands of hobby insiders. One photo wound up at BMW Sportscards, the Madison, Wisconsin, vintage-card business run by brothers Brian and Michael Wentz. Brian Wentz is portly, while Michael is thin, but they otherwise look remarkably alike— both are tall, with a mop of straight brown hair. Both wear rimless glasses and have piercing eyes. In hobby circles the Wentz brothers are known as humorless and argumentative men who can turn even mundane situations into confrontations. They had a falling-out with Mastro in the early 1990s, and they've been eager to settle the score ever since.

The Wentz brothers had told other dealers for years that the photo of The Card would be a powerful weapon against Mastro, who has even more money and resources than they do. They told hobby insiders they would use the photo as the centerpiece of a book or lawsuit against Mastro, but ultimately they never dropped the bomb. "A lot of people say we have an ax to grind, but we have no ax to grind with anyone," Brian Wentz said. "We've buried the hatchet."

Wentz pointed out that the photo is hardly concrete evidence that the Gretzky T206 Wagner was altered anyway. The Card does appear to be misshapen in the photo, but that may be an illusion created by a cheap camera. Another prominent T206 collector has a photocopy of Ray's picture, and, like the Wentz brothers, he won't go public with it. It's easy to manipulate Xeroxed images, he said, and he wouldn't want to pass off a doctored photocopy as evidence that the Gretzky T206 Wagner had been altered.

A veteran dealer acknowledged that he, too, got a copy of the photo, courtesy of Bob Sevchuk. He was tempted to use the picture to stick it to Mastro, but the blowback might be worse than any damage done to Mastro's reputation. Besides, if questions are raised about the hobby's top card, wouldn't that hurt business for everybody? If the million-dollar card turns out to be a fraud, what does that say about the cards people pick up for $50 or $100?

"I don't like Bill Mastro," the dealer said. "You could say I hate Bill Mastro. But in the end this would be more trouble than it is worth, and I don't want to get involved."

Tired of the battle, Ray eventually gave up his crusade and returned to his quiet life in New Jersey, refusing in recent years even to discuss The Card. If Sotheby's didn't care that it had sold an altered card—and McNall and Gretzky didn't care that they'd purchased an altered card—then why should Alan Ray care?

What happened to The Card after it was purchased from Ray has stoked the hobby rumor mill for two decades. Because Mastro is a larger-than-life figure in the world of collecting, the tales that surround him often take on preposterous proportions. Some say he took The Card home and put it under a bedpost to make it as smooth as possible. Or that maybe he took a scalpel to it. Some claimed that his home itself reflected his avocation—it looked like an obstacle course: Visitors had to maneuver around stacks of heavy books he'd placed on top of baseball cards to smooth out their wrinkles.

Whatever the case, Sevchuk and Ray said that one thing is certain: When the card later known as the T206 Wagner PSA NM-MT 8 returned to the public eye a few years after Mastro bought it at Sevchuk's Hicksville store, it had been altered. The edges were no longer wavy. The red printer's line was gone.

"Somebody," Ray said, "changed the card."

Mastro has always swatted away rumors that The Card had been altered, flying into a rage at the slightest suggestion that its bright colors, clean edges, and sharp corners are the result of skillful card surgery. "There's nothing wrong with that card!" Mastro once screamed during an interview. "There's nothing wrong with that card!"

THE CARD GETS A PEDIGREE

Wayne Gretzky and Bruce McNall might not have seen Alan Ray's letter warning that the baseball card they'd just spent $451,000 for at the Sotheby's auction was illegitimate. But plenty of other people were raising questions about The Card. Some of them were doing it on television before thousands of viewers.

Shortly after McNall and Gretzky bought their T206 Wagner, MS-NBC anchorman Keith Olbermann, then a broadcaster in Los Angeles, talked about the rumors that had dogged The Card one Sunday night on his KCBS-TV sports show. Olbermann's guest that evening, Beverly Hills Card Shop owner Matt Federgreen, said he had heard rumors that The Card was thinner than it should have been, possibly because it had been cut from a sheet and then trimmed to remove oversized, rounded edges.

"When you have a card that looks like the Hope Diamond, the first question you ask is, how did it hold up that well?" Olbermann said years later. "Unless you took it from the printing press and put it in a book for decades, it wouldn't hold up. Cards lose quality over time."

By then McNall was overwhelmed with buyer's remorse; he feared he and Gretzky had been fleeced for nearly a half million dollars.

"Right after we bought The Card, the press was all over it, and at the time people were saying it was trimmed," McNall remembered. "It bothered me. It was a concern. I called Sotheby's and said, 'What's the story here?' I was assured The Card was fine, and if it wasn't, they would undo the transaction. They said if something was improperly done, they would take care of it."

Fortunately for McNall, Gretzky, and their T206 Wagner, a new company that would revolutionize the way people collect trading cards was about to open the doors of its Southern California head-quarters. Professional Sports Authenticator was born in 1991, just a few months after McNall and Gretzky bought The Card. Its mission: Inspect trading cards for authenticity and award grades based on condition and appearance, protect consumers from the counterfeit-ers and card doctors who had turned the hobby into a roiling back-water. That was the stated mission anyway.

PSA's launch covered up a multitude of problems for Bill Mastro. He needed this card to be graded; he needed to have it declared au-thentic and high-grade. Mastro no longer owned The Card, but his fortunes were still linked to it. Mastro had sold the Wagner through its first big payday, and it had helped establish his reputation as a man to be reckoned with in the world of sports collectibles. The publicity The Card had generated would create millions of dollars' worth of free publicity for the hobby, just as it would for the auction house Mastro would open a few years later. He had a lot riding on The Card, and if the Wagner were trimmed, he would take the hit. His franchise was being threatened. Josh Evans remembered those days and the pressure that was building on Mastro.

"Look, McNall was saying, 'What the fuck? The card is trimmed?' Sotheby's was the agent—they didn't know," Evans said. "Copeland was the guy that bought the card from Mastro. Mastro set all this up.

He had to take care of it. He had to prove it was not trimmed and get it graded," said Evans.

Fortunately for Mastro, one of the first graders hired by PSA was Bill Hughes. Mastro and Hughes had known each other for years. Hughes was a well-known card and memorabilia dealer with weekly ads in *Sports Card Digest*, a visible face on the card-show circuit.

Evans even speculates that Mastro had a hand in picking Hughes to grade it. "I can hear him saying it now: 'I don't want no fucking talk about that card being trimmed. I want it to be fucking authentic.'"

The Gretzky T206 Wagner would become the first card ever examined by PSA, and the rumors that had swirled around it for years seemed to settle once the company declared The Card authentic, graded it PSA 8, and slabbed it between two pieces of clear plastic. "Once they put it between the plastic, it removed the questions," Olbermann said of the way most people viewed the grading process and the graders who would become known as "slabbers."

But the questions were not removed from the minds of many, including Olbermann. "You want to know what I think about slabbers?" he asked. "Homer Simpson is the safety expert at the Springfield nuclear plant. That's what I think of slabbers."

The slabbers hired by PSA to grade The Card were hardly characters from a cartoon show. Hughes was well known as a master card doctor, refined in the art of restoration. His partner, Mervin Lee, was even better. They were described by one collector as "two thieves in the night," adept at buying collections at shows and flea markets, then restoring and selling them at a much higher price. Hughes once described Lee to a friend as having "the eye of a magician." When others looked at a collection and saw a pile of old cards, Lee saw possibilities. He could see things nobody else could see.

"I sat at a table with Bill and Mervin at a show in Long Beach in the early nineties, and Mervin showed me cards he doctored," said Shelly Jaffe, the veteran sports collectibles dealer who was arrested during Operation Bullpen, an FBI investigation into forged autographs and counterfeit memorabilia. (Jaffe has since become an expert consultant for the FBI on forgies and counterfeits and has worked with HBO and other media investigating forgeries.) "Mervin would buy cards at the show and come back to the table and say, 'Bill, we can turn this from bronze to gold.'"

Of course, this was not necessarily a bad thing in the minds of collectors and the new boys on the block—the graders. You had to know what you were grading and whether it had been doctored before you could assign it a grade—and there was no one better to make that diagnosis than the doctor himself.

As Josh Evans said, "There were not too many people who had the imprimatur to do that kind of work."

Hughes dances around the issue of card doctoring: Certainly, he has heard the rumors, which he dismisses as a result of the gossipy, jealous nature of the hobby.

"I've heard the stories," he said. "I can't counter [the rumors]. People point the finger at me and at Mervin and at Mastro. If you're a high-profile person in this hobby, you are a target. If it's that easy to make money doctoring cards, how come I'm no longer a major card dealer?"

Hughes now runs his own auction house in Flower Mound, Texas, selling comic books, movie posters, and baseball cards. But in 1991 he focused primarily on cards. He would later describe the scene around The Card as he and Lee examined it at PSA's office in Santa Ana, California.

"I do recall holding it. There were about fifteen people standing behind me when we were encapsulating it," he said. "I had learned how to use the encapsulation machine, but I had never used it. I remember worrying about lining up the card, hoping I didn't misalign it. I remember joking about it. The thing I joke about now is that that card will forever have my thumbprint on it. I had to hold it to grade it."

Mervin Lee remembered how nervous they all were, how they dreaded handling the fragile piece of paper brought to them by a "guy named Chris" from Superior Galleries, McNall's gallery in Beverly Hills. Joined by a third grader, Hughes and Lee were struck by the condition and the color of The Card. The three agreed on a NM-MT 8 (near-mint to mint, grade eight of ten) without much discussion. The grading process usually involves two graders and a third who serves as a tiebreaker: If the two agree on the grade, the process continues and the card is slabbed; if there is a disagreement, the third person breaks the tie.

"My recollection was that it was pretty unanimous," Lee said. "It had an amazing look to it. It was really a beautiful card. At the time I think there were corner problems. There are a lot of cards in PSA 8 holders that look like mint cards, but when you look more closely, you understand why it got an eight."

The world would find out, in the spring of 1991, that the Gretzky T206 Honus Wagner was in the best condition of any Wagner card known to exist in the world—PSA would give it an 8 NM-MT, the highest grade a Wagner has ever received.

Mastro had his grade—and it was worth a fortune.

Still, the rumors wouldn't go away.

Even before PSA graded the Gretzky T206 Honus Wagner in 1991, the once-innocent world of trading cards was being transformed into a lawless frontier filled with counterfeiters, card doctors, and hustlers. But before the mid-1970s, before the value of old baseball cards skyrocketed, the hobby was a genteel pastime dominated by baseball-crazy kids and slightly eccentric men. They sometimes had little in common besides their need for old baseball cards. They were isolated islands of obsession drizzled across the country, only occasionally meeting face-to-face or speaking on the telephone. They communicated primarily through letters, mimeographed newsletters, and classified ads in the *Sporting News* and other sports publications. Transactions rarely involved more than a few bucks, and bartering was common.

Bill Mastro's early years in the hobby are a testament to the simplicity and camaraderie of the hobby back then. Like many Baby Boomers, Mastro became addicted to baseball cards as a kid. He grew up in rural New Jersey playing baseball in his backyard with his younger brother, Randy, who would become a politically connected attorney who served as deputy mayor of New York City during Rudy Giuliani's tenure. Unlike the other kids who lost interest in baseball cards as they discovered Lennon or Dylan or pot or the antiwar movement, Mastro found time for his cards, along with sex, drugs, and rock 'n' roll.

Mastro has an obscure third-string catcher named Bob Schmidt to thank for the empire he lords over today. By 1965, twelve-year-old Mastro was already a compulsive collector who organized his cards numerically in shoe boxes and dresser drawers and kept checklists of the cards he owned. "I was always a collector," he said. "You either have it or you don't. There's a gene we collectors are born with, and I save everything—comic books, baseball cards—all sorts of things."

In the summer of '65, Mastro would have done just about anything to collect every one of the 572 cards Topps issued that year. He pulled weeds and gathered up soda bottles to trade them in for their nickel deposit. He did enough to buy more than two thousand packs of baseball cards that summer. But one card proved impossibly elusive: the card featuring Schmidt, the backup catcher for the New York Yankees. No matter how many packs Mastro bought, Schmidt was nowhere to be found. The New Jersey summer eased into autumn, and the local candy store stopped stocking baseball cards and started to sell football cards.

The setback forced Mastro to look for other ways to track down Schmidt. In the back of the *Sporting News,* Mastro found an ad for Woody Gelman's Card Collectors Company of Franklin Square, New York. "Send 15-cent stamp and quarter to get catalogue," the ad said. Mastro ordered the Schmidt card from Gelman, the Topps artist who designed the company's famed 1952 card series and helped create Bazooka Joe, the hero of Bazooka gum comics. The catalog, however, was what changed Mastro's life. It opened up a whole new world—it featured thousands of old Goudey, Bowman, Topps, and T206 cards. "It blew me away to learn there were cards made in the 1940s and before," Mastro said. "I loved those old cards. They fascinated me."

The Gelman catalog also led Mastro to a small grassroots network of hard-core collectors. "I really found the collecting of cards to be a hobby in 1965," Mastro said. "There were a few guys who advertised in these small ads in the *Sporting News.* Most of them were just interested in trading cards. They would put out these mimeographed lists to about two hundred people of what they were looking for or had to trade. Very few people sold cards back then."

Mastro befriended men like Frank Nagy, the Detroit pipe fitter who had one of the largest collections in the nation, numbering in the tens of thousands of cards, some of which dated back to the 1880s. Nagy would raise money for new cards by auctioning off his doubles through a newsletter sent to several hundred customers six times a year. He was a prolific letter writer who delighted in sharing his knowledge with kids like Mastro.

"I first wrote Nagy in 1966, at the age of fourteen, and he immediately recognized how lost I was in this hobby of old men," Mastro wrote in a catalog description for Nagy's T206 Wagner his auction house sold for $456,000 in December 2005. "He took the time to write me long, multipage letters, guiding me on how to collect. He encouraged me. He promoted the hobby as a uniting family activity. He took the time to teach this fourteen-year-old kid the ropes.

"Early on in our hobby, when the conventions started, everybody clamored to get over to Nagy's, to see the collection and do some trading," Mastro added. "Only problem was, none of us had anything he needed! But that didn't stop him from sending us home with boxes full of goodies. No one ever left empty-handed. He so enjoyed seeing collectors full of enthusiasm for their hobby. I remember him saying to just send him some stuff when you got something good. Everyone loved Big Frank. He was like Santa Claus, only better."

Mastro was at the hobby's first organized convention, held in 1969 in the upstate New York basement of longtime dealer Mike Aronstein. Card shows soon became regular events, and Mastro was a fixture at those early conventions. "It was such a great time," he said. "Guys came from all over the country with cards other guys had never seen before. Believe me, it was a lovefest!

"It was so different back then. There were no price guides. It wasn't about money. It was about the hunt. What you needed. The art of the deal when it came to trading. Watching how deals were made. It was so much fun back then."

Those fun days would prove to be as elusive as a .400 hitter. The struggling Major League Baseball Players Association would use baseball cards to fill its coffers, turning it into one of the most powerful unions in the history of organized labor even as it ended Topps' long stranglehold on the new cards. A new class of collectors sprang up, and this group saw cards more as investments than as art.

Especially troubling was the rise in bogus and restored cards. As prices for old and new cards rose by leaps and bounds, altered and counterfeited cards became increasingly profitable. The hobby, once a small, self-policed group of gentlemen collectors, was suddenly an eat-or-be-eaten jungle.

Seemingly overnight, baseball cards would become worth big money. Two of the biggest beneficiaries were Bill Mastro and The Card.

MARVIN MONEY

By 1991 the innocent days of the hobby were long over. Marvin Miller, hired as the first executive director of the fledgling Major League Baseball Players Association in 1966, inadvertently initiated the beginning of the end when he took on Topps, the Brooklyn candy company that had monopolized the baseball-card business since the 1950s. Miller is the man largely responsible for the wealth the players now enjoy, for their fat contracts, and for their power against management. He forged the unity and strength the Players Association has flexed time and time again in its battles against Major League Baseball and its owners. But in 1966 the players were getting peanuts from Topps.

There were no iPods, no Xboxes, no Internet. There were baseball cards—and kids acquired them by the bushel, flipping them in school lots and amassing huge collections. In a dusty little office in New York City's Biltmore Hotel, Miller was making a shocking discovery: the millions of dollars generated by the gum manufacturer who packaged those baseball cards along with its powdery, brittle confections were going almost exclusively to Topps. While Topps was raking in the dough off the players' images, the players themselves were being paid a paltry $125 bonus—and they were happy to get it.

Miller laughed at the incongruity. Today he is seen as the most influential union man in sports history, but in 1966 he was a young organizer, the first executive director of the Players Association, working out of the office of the onetime traveling secretary for the New York Yankees, Frank Scott, who had become a licensing agent. Miller discovered a stack of contracts lying on one of the two old battered file cabinets in the office, and, he said, "I was appalled by the tactics the company was using. They had scouting crews and would scout minor-league players who weren't likely to make the majors. They'd offer them $5 to sign, and the contract provided Topps exclusive rights to the player's signature and picture. They were five-year contracts that would begin when the player became a major leaguer." The contracts reminded Miller of what the players were up against—it was like the reserve-clause battle he would eventually fight, only in a different format.

Thanks to Sy Berger, who worked in the Topps promotions department, almost every major leaguer had a contract with the company. Berger had parlayed his connections to the Shorin family, which owned Topps, through Joel Shorin, a fraternity brother of Berger's at Bucknell. Shorin would become president of Topps and would turn the company into a virtual baseball-card monopoly for them. Berger toured spring-training clubhouses bearing gifts and free dinners. He became a ubiquitous presence around baseball, carrying around a catalog—Miller described it as an "S&H Green Stamp kind of book with lawn hoses and toolboxes"—that also contained television sets and refrigerators, giving the players the option of taking the cash or bringing home a new vacuum cleaner. Miller would find that just about every player in the game had a Topps deal.

He devised a strategy and put it in motion: He would employ the same tactics as Berger to get his players to understand that they needed a better deal—clubhouse by clubhouse, player by player, Miller would rebuild the players' endorsement business. But first he had to convince his board that he wasn't insane.

"We had no money, no office, no staff, and a dues structure of $50 a member," Miller said of his first big fight on behalf of the players. "We had an immediate financial problem. I was looking at every-thing that might produce revenue. I sat down with the players on the executive board and gave them the results of my findings. I wasn't an expert on licensing, but it seemed to me the kind of revenue Topps was generating wasn't in line with that $125 fee and $5 bonus."

Miller had discovered exactly what the revenues were through court papers in an antitrust complaint that the Fleer gum company had filed against Topps—and they were easily in the millions.

Miller still relishes talking about the Topps deal. Nearing ninety in the winter of 2006, he sat in an upscale fish restaurant on the East Side of Manhattan, a glass of whiskey in his hand and a teasing smile on his still-handsome face, as he recounted the details of his strategy and his ultimate victory. His blue eyes sparkled as he rubbed a finger across his slight mustache.

But that day forty years ago during the meeting with the players on his board, he was anything but sardonic. Miller had just come out of a meeting with Shorin—a famous meeting, as it turns out, during which Shorin uttered one of the memorable lines in baseball's long history. Miller had set up an appointment with Shorin, who had come to the union's new office at 375 Park (still a lowly office, said Miller, but bet-ter than Frank Scott's room in the Biltmore), and Miller had set about telling the Topps boss his concerns about the company's arrangement with the players.

"He was a likable man," Miller said. "He heard me out without an interruption. I said we were prepared to negotiate. Then he looked at me, and with a straight face he said, 'I really don't see your muscle.' He had these five-year contracts staggered in his favor. He just explained the facts of life to me and said, 'Frankly, I don't see any reason we should change.' "

Miller did what he does best—figured out a strategy. He had discovered that celebrities usually got a percentage of sales for endorsements and went to his board with his plan.

"I told them Topps wasn't running a charity," he said. "I told them, 'It's a business. That they'd taken advantage of a lack of experience of kids who played baseball. In a dog-eat-dog world, that is not unusual. Some of the minor leaguers had signed when they weren't even twenty-one.' The players said, 'How do we attack this?'

"I told them I would give them the pros and cons."

No player would renew a contract, first of all. When Topps would approach at the three-year point with an offer of renewal, the player would decline. The downside, of course, was that the player wouldn't get the $75 renewal fee or the $125, and until the union had enough refusals, they really wouldn't have muscle.

"I told them it could take so long that many of them wouldn't be in baseball," Miller said. "But I told them, 'Eventually we'll beat it. It's too lucrative for that company to walk away.' "

The board approved Miller's plan unanimously—and Marvin Miller would later use the same tactics he used against Topps in securing a collective-bargaining agreement between the owners and players.

When the company got wind of Miller's tactics, Berger sprang into action, working on the players, although by the end of that first spring training, Topps was shaken enough that Miller got a call from Shorin—the call he'd been waiting for.

"I want to start by saying, 'I see your muscle,' " the Topps boss told Miller.

Miller smiled again as he told the story, one that has become part of the lore of baseball. On November 19, 1968, Topps and the Players Association agreed on a deal that would double the signing bonus to $250 and give the players 8 percent of all sales under $4 million and 10 percent of sales over $4 million. The revenue that first year came to $320,000.

By 1972, Miller had amassed a war chest for the players in anticipation of fierce battles with the owners over licensing, revenue, player movement, and salaries. Even before he took on Topps, he'd secured a deal with Coca-Cola that gave the soft-drink bottler the right to use the pictures of players on the undersides of bottle caps. In return, the union would get $60,000 a year, money that Miller would distribute in spring training, beginning in 1968, along with the card money. (The players began referring to the bonus money as "Marvin Money.")

But Miller was nothing if not prudent, and he began decreasing licensing shares to players in anticipation of a strike. "We did not have to raise a dollar for the '72 strike," Miller said of the twelve-day shutdown. And that would hold true all the way through the fifty-day 1981 strike and the brutal 1994 lockout. By 1994 the players had a $175 million war chest, 90 percent of which had come through the sale of baseball cards. Marvin Money had gone from $100 per player in 1968 to $80,000 in 1991.

"Think of yourself as being a member of management," Miller said. "And ask yourself, 'Should we take a tack on a lockout on the theory of starving the union out? Is it a union with no bankroll, no income other than players' salaries? Or is it a union with a source of income?'"

The owners would finally figure out that the players were making a fortune off licensing and would create the marketing and promotions arm of MLB that exists today. But thanks to Miller and the deals he sealed, MLB still cannot market a player's image for commercial purposes, a concept the owners had some trouble accepting.

"They have cheated," Miller said with a smile. "I remember Walter O'Malley was using players' pictures on glasses or mugs with a gasoline chain to promote gasoline. I got wind of it. I was in Vero Beach—I had become fairly friendly with O'Malley—and he said, 'These players are our players.' "

I reminded him, "Walter, they're under contract to play baseball for you."

Fittingly, Miller has his own baseball card, with his picture on it, and fans often send him autograph requests in the mail. He signs them and sends them back. Not a week goes by that he doesn't get a request for an autograph. Of course, the fact that he used the sale of players' images to fans to fund work stoppages is undoubtedly lost on most of his correspondents, a delicious irony that Miller himself surely secretly enjoys. But he also knows this: He saw the value.

"When I was a child, I had baseball cards," he said. "On the underside of cups of ice cream there were baseball players, actors, Broadway people. Unlike the people who tell you their mothers threw them away, I don't know what happened to mine. And it's too bad."

As for his own card, you can pick that up on eBay. And how much is it worth?

"Oh," said Miller, "maybe three cents."

The value of the card industry to baseball players would evolve over the years, through a series of antitrust suits involving the players, Topps, and Fleer, including a bizarre suit in which the players and Topps were named as codefendants in restraining other card companies from competing in the card business. Fleer, the Philadel-

phia firm that had perfected the formula for bubble gum years earlier, had long been eager to jump into the baseball-card market. But
Topps' contract with the Players Association required the union to
get the gum company's permission before it agreed to license any
product that featured players' likenesses, and Shorin and his staff
made it clear they would not open the door for competitors interested in issuing full-length sets, especially if the cards came with
gum. Topps had been synonymous with baseball cards for almost
twenty years, and Shorin wasn't about to give that exclusivity away.

But U.S. District Court Judge Clarence Newcomer found that
Topps and the Players Association had indeed restrained trade in vio-
lation of the Sherman Antitrust Act, writing that "Topps' rights are
not protected by patents or copyrights. There is no legal requirement
that either Topps or an individual enter into an exclusive, as opposed
to a non-exclusive, contract for the use of the player's picture. Topps
did not have its market position thrust upon it." Newcomer also
found that Topps' contracts contained numerous restrictive clauses
and that Topps' only competition was the Players Association.

"The judge was an idiot," Miller said flatly.

And certainly, his ruling against Topps and the Players Association would end up benefiting the players as much as any decision in
the history of the game ever had. It opened up the market for baseball cards. Suddenly the players were entertaining offers. "Which is
what we wanted to do," Miller said, although at the time he was a
little less enthusiastic about the ruling. "The next thing you know,
we're getting bids from three companies. I had no desire to be labeled an antitrust violator, but . . . we had our cake and ate it, too."

The appeals court would eventually overturn the ruling, but the
horse was out of the corral.

Fleer Corp. v. Topps Chewing Gum, Inc. opened the door for new companies to jump into the card market, and Fleer and Donruss—a Memphis-based company then best known for the cards it manufactured for *The Six Million Dollar Man, Dallas, The Dukes of Hazzard*, and other TV shows—offered the Players Association more profitable terms than those offered by Topps. In 1981 the union raked in an additional $600,000 from baseball cards from all three companies.

The rookie companies had just a few months to print and deliver cards before the 1981 season began, and in the rush to market, both companies made dozens of laughably embarrassing mistakes. Donruss noted that Bobby Bonds of the St. Louis Cardinals had 986 career home runs, 231 more than Hank Aaron's record 755. The card for Houston's Vern Ruhle actually featured a picture of his teammate Frank LaCorte. Fleer, meanwhile, identified Yankee All-Star Graig Nettles as "Craig," the Giants' Darrell Evans as "Derrell," and Dodgers rookie Fernando Valenzuela as "Fernand."

Fleer and Donruss fixed the mistakes, setting off a gold rush for the error cards and the corrected versions. Collectors scrambled for both, figuring that either version would be rarer than cards printed consistently through their press runs. Soon both versions of the Nettles card were worth $20.

By the time Judge Newcomer's ruling was overturned, the Players Association had allied itself with Fleer and Donruss, and for good reason. Sales of cards had exploded; according to some estimates, the card market had expanded by 80 percent. Fleer, Donruss, and the players found an easy way to get around Topps' agreement with the union: They simply didn't include gum with the cards. Topps, exhausted by its five-year legal battle and wary of tangling with Miller and the players again, decided not to fight back. Besides, there was enough money to be made for everyone. By the early nineties, annual sales of new trading cards would reach $1 billion.

Meanwhile, prices for older cards were also beginning to sky-rocket. Those early card shows started drawing bigger crowds, and the new collectors brought with them a new attitude toward collect-ing. They didn't stay up all night after shows talking about the mer-its of the Old Judge set or Cracker Jack cards. This new crowd saw baseball cards as underappreciated investment opportunities, and they jumped into the hobby looking to make a profit. Many were drawn to the hobby after reading about the sale of three 1952 Mickey Mantle cards at the Philadelphia Card and Sports Memorabilia Show in March 1980. The card has always had star quality for collectors, and not only because it featured the greatest player of the 1950s. Like the T206 Wagner, it also came with a great story. Before 1974, Topps had staggered the release dates of its cards in order to main-tain interest throughout the baseball season. The Mantle card was one of the cards in the last set released in 1952, and many store own-ers, still trying to sell earlier releases, declined to buy them. Topps got stuck with so many of these late-issue cards that it eventually hired a garbage scow to dump several tons of them—including God knows how many Mantles—into the Atlantic Ocean.

The Mantle card sold for about $700 in 1980, but two young card dealers named Rob Barsky and Bob Cohen paid an astonishing $3,100 for one Mantle and $3,000 each for two more at an auction at the Philadelphia show. Hobby insiders couldn't believe it—some wondered if Barsky and Cohen were lunatics. Others wondered if they were onto something no one else had figured out.

Few collectors had been particularly excited about rookie cards in the past, but thanks to Barsky and Cohen many began to look at them with the eye of a Wall Street trader: buy low, sell high. Some tried to scoop up old rookie cards of already-established players such as Pete Rose. Others tried to buy up new cards featuring emerging

new stars—Valenzuela and Yankee first baseman Don Mattingly—
who showed star potential. Thanks to "rookiemania," the prices of
cards went through the roof. By the end of the 1984 season, Donruss's Mattingly card was worth $20, and the entire set sold for $80—
$66 more than it had gone for at the beginning of the season.

National sports and finance magazines touted baseball cards as
terrific investments. In the long run, it would be a foolish claim. The
values of cards, like any commodity, are dictated by supply and demand; 1952 Mantle cards were rare and valuable because Topps and
early-fifties collectors didn't save them. With so many collectors
now saving so many cards, the values of all those Valenzuela and
Mattingly cards weren't likely to increase the way the 1952 Mantle
cards had. But in the short haul, the magazines were right—in June
1988, *Money* magazine reported that baseball cards had a 42.5 percent compound average return, compared to 14 percent for corporate bonds and 12.7 percent for common stocks. Cards had become
a commodity.

The scent of money was everywhere, and the predators were right
behind the herd of speculators hoping to get rich on baseball cards.
Reprints that cost pennies to make could be sold to the gullible and
the greedy for $10, $15, $20, or more. The risks were not significant;
trading-card counterfeiting was hardly a priority for law-enforcement
officials. The market was soon flooded with counterfeits; counterfeiting became so ubiquitous that when Upper Deck, now the hobby's
leading card manufacturer, was created in 1988, it used security as an
advertising talking point. The company boasted it had developed in-
novations that prevented counterfeiting. (Upper Deck would later be
embroiled in its own scandals. The company has been accused of reprinting rare error cards and limited editions so its executives could
sell them for huge profits on the secondary market. According to Pete

Williams in *Card Sharks,* the reprinting would occur months after the original press run, long after the public believed production had stopped. Upper Deck would then distribute the cards to board members and executives, a practice that came to light when a former card-shop owner named Bill Hemrick, who had been a founding director of the company and still had a small stake in it, filed a $10 million lawsuit alleging the "secret manufacturing and distribution to themselves of various sports trading cards," among other claims.)

Rising prices for vintage cards, too, drew the attention of counterfeiters and card doctors. The time was ripe for neutral, third-party services that could vouch for a card's authenticity, grade it to determine its value, and give peace of mind to collectors.

The time was ripe for Professional Sports Authenticator.

PSA AND THE DOCTORS

PSA is a division of a publicly held company called Collectors Universe, whose roots date back to 1986, when CU president David Hall founded Professional Coin Grading Service, a firm that authenticates and grades collectible coins. Hall was convinced that card collectors were also eager for a way to authenticate their purchases. So in 1991 he branched out into trading cards with PSA; since then Collectors Universe has expanded to stamp, paper currency, diamonds, and autograph authentication. The potential for growth remains enormous: In its annual report for 2005, Collectors Universe said it is considering expanding into comic books, jewelry, postcards, rare books, and musical instruments, among other markets.

Hall wanted to kick off the debut of Professional Sports Authenticator with a bang, and, thanks to the Gretzky T206 Wagner, he found a way to do that. As he described it, he approached a friend who happened to be one of Bruce McNall's partners at Superior Galleries.

"I explained we were starting a grading card service for sports cards and would like to grade the Wagner," Hall said. "They seemed to think it was a great idea."

Hall disputed any suggestions that his graders, Bill Hughes and Mervin Lee, knew that The Card had been trimmed or altered. He adamantly countered any claim that it looked odd or too perfect with what he viewed as the gold standard for authenticity: Under magnification, he said, The Card does not appear to have been trimmed or altered in any way.

Hall has good reason to downplay any hint of impropriety regarding the grading of The Card, of course: His company's reputation is at stake. According to its Web site, PSA will not grade cards that "bear evidence of trimming, re-coloring, restoration, or any other forms of tampering." Two of PSA's leading competitors—Beckett Grading Services and Sportscard Guaranty Corporation (SGC)—also won't grade cards that have been altered. Global Authentication Incorporated (GAI), the other major grading service, will label cards that have been restored as "Authentic Only."

Further, PSA claims it will not grade trading cards that have been hand-cut from printers' sheets. The grading service will grade hand-cut cards if they couldn't be obtained any other way— from the back of a cereal box, for example—but not if they were traditionally cut at the factory and distributed in packs of cigarettes, tobacco, or gum. "PSA will not grade cards cut from sheets that can be obtained in a normal fashion," the Web site says. "For example, PSA will not grade a 1979 O-Pee-Chee Wayne Gretzky card cut from a sheet because that sheet was issued in non-sheet form."

Other companies followed PSA's lead, portraying themselves as marshals in a Wild West town that would devolve into lawlessness without their help, and in many ways the competition helped clean up the grading business. Although PSA remains the most prestigious grading service in the hobby—the company has become synonymous with card grading in the same way Kleenex has become synonymous with tissues—the other grading heavyweights forced PSA, which has graded more than 8 million cards since its inception, to alter its modus operandi.

"Things have changed with SGC and Beckett and GAI. They forced PSA to become honest," Jaffe said. "Beckett doesn't take any shit. Jim Beckett has been honest his entire life. He could have manipulated the market with his price guides and made a fortune, but he never did. He's one of the few honest guys in this business."

The Wagner card generated headlines and gossip but not much business for PSA—at least not at first. PSA lost about $10,000 a month, and former president Steve Rocchi remembers spending many frustrating weekends each month trying to convince dealers at card conventions of the need for an objective third-party grading service. In those early years, PSA graded about a thousand cards a month. But within a few years, business exploded, and by 1998, PSA was grading eighty thousand cards a month. And the slabbers weren't always looking closely. "Let's say a guy sends ten thousand pieces to be graded," said Jaffe, echoing what other collectors have said. "They were trying to get their business off the ground. They gave higher grades to people who gave them more business. They might not have done that for the guy who sent ten pieces in. This was like Mark McGwire and steroids. Everybody knew what was going on, but nobody wanted to say anything. Too many people were making money."

That wasn't the only criticism PSA faced. Partly because of its place in the industry, and partly because of its early practices, PSA had inspired ill will among collectors and dealers for years. Collectors blamed the company and its rivals for jacking up the prices of cards, because dealers pass the costs on to their customers. PSA's fees can be as low as $6 per card or as high as $150, depending on the age of the cards and how quickly collectors want their cards returned.

Collectors complained that higher grades are awarded to big-volume customers.

"The grading system has a million flaws," Lifson said. "Even if everyone's heart is pure and there is no corruption, it'd still be subjective."

Other collectors have said that grading services aren't consistent, that a card sent in one day might get a different grade from the same card sent in on another. "I didn't like the grade I received from PSA for a T206 card," one collector said. "I got a five, and I felt the card was a six. I cracked open the holder and sent it back. I got a PSA seven."

PSA's large volume of business may also have contributed to its reputation as being a card-grading assembly line. According to the Collectors Universe annual report, PSA's thirteen graders examined 1,084,000 cards in fiscal year 2005. Assuming that those graders work eight hours a day, five days a week, fifty-two weeks a year, they grade 320 cards a day. That means PSA's graders, on average, spend about ninety seconds on each card—assuming they never use the toilet, go on vacation, eat lunch, or take breaks to gab with co-workers around the watercooler.

Similar complaints have been lodged about other Collectors Universe companies. A lawsuit filed against Mastro Auctions and Collectors Universe in Boone County, Indiana, Superior Court in 2006 said that PSA/DNA, Collectors Universe's autograph-authentication division, rubber-stamped pieces it was hired to authenticate and grade prior to a Mastro auction. The plaintiff, a memorabilia dealer named Bill Daniels, spent $20,000 for more than two thousand autographed photos, including pictures of Mickey Mantle, Alex Rodriguez, Michael Jordan, and Wayne Gretzky. Daniels said most of the photos he purchased at the December 2004 Mastro Auctions sale had bent corners, creases, and smeared signatures. Some of the autographs, his suit contends, were forgeries. Daniels asked for a refund, and when the auction house refused, he filed suit against Mastro Auctions, Collectors Universe, and PSA/DNA.

During discovery Daniels learned that PSA's three-man authentication team spent about sixteen hours over two days reviewing thousands of items offered in Mastro's December 2004 auction. "That's just a few seconds per item," said Daniels's attorney, S. Andrew Burns. "That's not even enough time to move the photos from one stack to another."

Even more disturbing, Burns said, is that one of the PSA/DNA experts sent to Mastro's Illinois offices to offer an objective examination of the photos was Zach Rullo, the same man who consigned the photos to the auction. "That's a conflict of interest, absolutely," Burns said.

In June 2006, Judge Matthew C. Kincaid dismissed the case against Collectors Universe and PSA/DNA, because Daniels did not have a contract with the authentication service—PSA/DNA had been hired by Mastro Auctions, not Daniels. The judge allowed the case against Mastro Auctions, however, to proceed. "I'm going to keep fighting on behalf of everybody who has ever got screwed by these guys," Daniels said.

Like Daniels, Michael Gidwitz, too, believes that PSA and other grading services have failed to provide an adequate safety net. He flips through auction catalogs and hobby publications and is shocked at how many more high-quality cards are available these days compared to ten and twenty years ago. Some of those top-dollar cards, Gidwitz concedes, may have been dug out of attics and sock drawers as the value of old cards skyrocketed. But Gidwitz believes that most were trimmed, colored, or repaired before they were sold.

"It just doesn't make sense that there are so many more gem-mint and mint cards than there were in the past," Gidwitz said. "This is not right."

There is one possible explanation, Gidwitz said: Grading companies are slabbing cards that have been altered. Many of the cards that received what Gidwitz calls "plastic surgery," moreover, will never be detected. PSA and other services embed cards between two slabs of clear plastic after they are graded. There is no economic incentive to reexamine a "slabbed" card with a high grade, since it could be returned with a lower rating. It might even be rejected as altered.

The rumors surrounding the Gretzky T206 Wagner seemed to die down after Hall and his staff slabbed it. "To my eyes the Wagner card we graded is a fantastic card in every way," Hall said. "Most Wagners are very low-grade. This card is superb—no wrinkles or creases, great color, and wonderful eye appeal. The bottom line is that if you look at The Card out of the holder, there is no evidence of trimming. The edges look exactly like you would expect a high-grade T206 to look . . . both to the naked eye and under magnification."

Still, not everyone was convinced. A few weeks after the card was graded, Mike Gutierrez, a consultant for McNall's Superior Galleries, told the *Chicago Tribune* that he had some problems with the card. Regardless of PSA's opinion, The Card had been altered, he said. Gutierrez didn't know about the dealings between Mastro and Ray at the Hicksville store, but he knew by examining the card for McNall that it didn't look right. It certainly wasn't the "mint" card it was advertised to be.

"The card was definitely cut at some point," Gutierrez said. "I don't know when it was cut, or by whom, but it sure was. I have no doubt."

In one of those strange twists that make the field of sports collectibles seem so weird and incestuous to outsiders, Gutierrez was hired by Collectors Universe in September 2005 to work as an autograph authenticator.

FALL OF A KING

T he rumors that had dogged the Gretzky T206 Wagner subsided soon after PSA slabbed it, but by then Bruce McNall had much bigger problems than a questionable baseball card. The flamboyant businessman who once falsely boasted about being a teenage millionaire had been living large on other people's money for years, and by the early 1990s it had become apparent to creditors—and, soon enough, prosecutors—that Bruce McNall's oversized charisma and ambition dwarfed his resources. McNall, constantly struggling with a cash flow that just couldn't keep up with his expenses, had borrowed huge sums of money for nearly a decade by cooking his books and lying to banks.

McNall held off the inevitable for an impressive number of years, and even prosecutors expressed a grudging respect for his ability to hold the banks and the creditors at bay for so long. "A ten-year period without discovery," Assistant U.S. Attorney Peter Spivack said, "is pretty extraordinary."

As with so many things McNall did in his life, he bought the T206 Wagner because it was a one-of-a-kind piece—not unlike Gretzky himself—that he could show off to friends and business associates, another collectible to prove to others that he was rich and important.

Most people would think long and hard before spending that kind of money on a baseball card. But *GQ* magazine estimated that the California mogul laid out $465,000 a month on personal expenses alone, including $146,000 in house payments, $20,000 for gifts, $8,000 for helicopter costs, $25,000 in walking-around money, and a $2,000 allowance for flowers. For Bruce McNall, $451,000 was chump change.

McNall couldn't maintain that lifestyle forever, though, and by the early 1990s he was being peppered by lawsuits demanding payment. He sold the team's Boeing 727 through his Upper Deck Authenticated, which listed the plane, unbelievably, as an "autographed" item. The lavish gifts to players and employees dried up. The Kings even had to turn off the heat in their Van Nuys practice facility to save money. Vendors refused to do business with the team unless the Kings paid up front with cash or certified check. The game was over, and, in May 1994, McNall was forced to sell the majority share of the team. He filed for bankruptcy a few weeks later.

Federal prosecutors charged McNall in November 1994 with defrauding six banks of more than $236 million over ten years. The Department of Justice crafted the terms of the indictment with McNall's lawyers, and in return the coin king quickly pleaded guilty to conspiracy, wire fraud, and two counts of bank fraud.

Prosecutors said McNall obtained massive loans from banks by falsifying tax returns and financial statements; they also claimed that McNall and his staff created fake invoices for horses, coins, and other commodities offered as collateral for the loans. Like everything McNall did, this was an outrageous, larger-than-life scheme, and even though it was terribly illegal and involved huge amounts of other people's money, people found it hard not to be in awe of his chutzpah.

Employees of McNall Sports and Entertainment, for example, admitted they washed replicas of famous jerseys with stones and stained them with coffee and tea to make them look worn, then presented them to banks as authentic, game-used uniforms. McNall claimed that one load of "game-used jerseys" offered as collateral for a loan was worth $300,000; the jerseys were actually purchased for $200. One bank lent McNall money based on information provided by a horse appraiser. The appraiser, however, was McNall's chauffeur. McNall obtained another loan by putting up several horses. Unfortunately, he didn't own all of them, and the ones he did own were dead.

Prosecutors also said that McNall's employees switched labels on a rare-coin collection to give the impression it was owned by McNall. The coin king, however, was only managing the collection for Merrill Lynch. McNall's famous generosity, meanwhile, was extended to bank officials: He improperly loaned $50,000 to a Bank of America officer and bribed officials at other banks to win their favor.

McNall even stung his pal Gretzky. The Kings owner pledged a horse they owned together, Honor Grades, as collateral on an $850,000 loan without telling his star player. But Gretzky was a loyal partner and stood by McNall even after he was sentenced in January 1997 to seventy months in prison and ordered to repay $5 million. The Great One visited him in jail and defended his former employer in interviews. He even refused to let the Kings retire his number until McNall, released in 2001 with thirteen months sliced off his sentence for good behavior, could attend the ceremony.

The Card had been stored in Gretzky's safe-deposit box ever since McNall's troubles surfaced, and, like McNall's other assets, it was placed under the control of a trustee after McNall filed for bankruptcy protection. Gretzky bid $225,000 for McNall's share at a brief bankruptcy hearing in Los Angeles four years after he and McNall first purchased it at that wild and woolly Sotheby's auction. No other bids were submitted.

"Wayne had been a baseball fan all his life," Gretzky attorney Ron Fujikawa said after U.S. bankruptcy judge Lisa Fenning approved the sale. "I think he views it as an investment that could appreciate in value."

Actually, Gretzky didn't wait long enough to find out. A few months after the hearing, he sold The Card for a little over $500,000 to Treat Entertainment, the trading-card distributor that stocked cards at more than two thousand Wal-Mart stores across the country.

McNall and Gretzky, the men who gave The Card glamour and glitz, the men who gave it an incredible backstory, were the biggest losers in The Card sweepstakes, even bigger than Alan Ray. They are the only former owners of the Gretzky T206 Wagner who didn't reap huge returns. Gretzky probably lost money after expenses were deducted. At least Ray made a few bucks.

Treat Entertainment was about to put The Card to work. The Gretzky T206 Wagner would no longer be a rich man's plaything. Baseball Hall of Famers Brooks Robinson and Reggie Jackson, New York Knicks legend Walt Frazier, and actor Jim Belushi appeared at a New York press conference to kick off the "World's Most Valuable Trading Card Giveaway," a four-month promotion that would end with a live raffle on CNN's *Larry King Weekend*. The Gretzky T206 Wagner would be the grand prize, and one person, one average Joe, one lucky Wal-Mart shopper, would win a card worth more than a half million dollars.

The Holy Grail had become a sweepstakes prize, nothing more than the hook of a sales pitch, a capitalist's tool. It was shilling for Wal-Mart, the monster retail chain that by then had become for many people a symbol of the excesses of globalization and twenty-first-century big business. Wal-Mart had become a place where you could buy baseball cards, along with everything from TVs to jeans and potato chips. The little corner store with bubble-gum-dusted packs of cards had given way to the giant retailer, just as the hardware and sporting-goods and auto-parts stores and even the little dress shops on Main Street had been swallowed up by the big box. Honus Wagner's roots ran deep in his hometown of Carnegie, Pennsylvania. It is difficult to say how the Flying Dutchman would have felt about having his image used to promote a retail chain that has long been accused of paying substandard wages, destroying small-town shopping districts, and driving thousands of mom-and-pop stores out of business. He didn't want his picture used to sell cigarettes—but he was also a staunch supporter of free enterprise, a pro-business Republican.

But for Wal-Mart, Treat Entertainment, and the card manufacturers that sponsored the World's Most Valuable Trading Card Giveaway, this was about more than just selling baseball cards or a sales promotion. This was about restoring America's faith in baseball cards. It was about saving the hobby.

By the time Treat Entertainment bought the Gretzky T206 Wagner, the trading-card industry had begun a long decline. Upper Deck did for baseball cards what Starbucks did for coffee—it took an inexpensive everyday consumer product and turned it into a high-end status symbol. Upper Deck printed its cards on glossy cardboard stock, with crisp color photos of the players on both front and back and a trademark hologram to prevent counterfeiting. The retail price more than compensated for the higher production: At a time when Topps was selling cards for 50 cents a pack and $25 a set, Upper Deck cards sold for $1 or more a pack, while a full Upper Deck set cost $49.

Topps and other manufacturers quickly issued their own premium card series, and card sales exploded. In 1991, the same year McNall and Gretzky made international headlines by purchasing their T206 Wagner, collectors spent a record $1.2 billion on new trading cards.

In their rush to capitalize on consumers' surging demand for sports cards, however, the manufacturers violated the basic law of supply and demand—they made too many cards. There were too many brands, too many sets, for all but the most hard-core collectors to keep up. From the beginning of the 1995 baseball season through the 1995–96 NBA season, seven trading-card manufacturers issued 105 different sets of sports cards. Fleer alone printed nearly 2 billion cards a year during the boom times.

Skyrocketing card prices, meanwhile, made cards too rich for kids and casual fans—people might be willing to pay $5 for a venti cappuccino, but many drew the line at $5 baseball cards. Sales of new cards dropped 23 percent, to $850 million in 1993, and Wal-Mart and other giant retailers returned thousands of cases of unsold cards to manufacturers. Mom-and-pop card shops who didn't have Wal-Mart's leverage with manufacturers were forced to eat their losses, and many went out of business.

Then came the 1994 baseball strike. The collective-bargaining agreement between Major League Baseball and the Players Association expired on December 31, 1993, and the owners, eager to rein in labor costs, demanded a salary cap and an end to salary arbitration. The union was adamantly opposed to any management-imposed limits on player earnings. Negotiations went nowhere; both sides became more hostile and entrenched as the 1994 season dragged on. Finally, on August 12, 1994, the Major League Baseball Players Association went on strike, bolstered by a $175 million war chest—

Nelson, 3d B.; Martin, R. F.; Swandell, 2d B.; Eggler, C. F.;
E. Mills, 1st B.; Hatfield, S. S.; C. Mills, C.; Wolters, P.; Patterson, L. F.

THE MUTUAL (Green Stockings) B. B. CLUB OF NEW YORK.

New York City sporting goods company Peck & Snyder was responsible for the first baseball cards mass-produced for commercial purposes. The cards featured baseball teams—such as the Mutuals of New York—on one side and a Peck & Snyder advertisement on the other side. The cards were distributed on street corners. *(Robert Edward Auctions LLC)*

MAGIE, PHILA. NAT'L

NAPOLEON (LARRY) LAJOIE

PLANK, PHILA. AMER.

The T206 Honus Wagner isn't the only hurdle serious collectors have to overcome to complete the turn-of-the-century series. The Phillies' Sherry Magee was one of the National League's best hitters for years, but the printers still identified him as "Magie," and cards with his misspelled name are extremely difficult to find. Nobody really knows why pitcher Eddie Plank's card is so rare, although some speculate that Plank, like Wagner, may have objected to the use of his image on a tobacco card. The Goudey Gum Company meanwhile drove collectors crazy in 1933: The company said 240 cards were in its set, but only issued 239; a card was intentionally withheld to keep customers coming back. Goudey issued a card featuring the retired Napoleon Lajoie the following year, after collectors complained. *(Robert Edward Auctions LLC)*

The years just prior to World War I were a golden age for baseball cards as tobacco companies tried to top each other. This is an advertisement for the elaborate cards offered by the Hassan Cigarette Company—triple-folded cards that offered a baseball action scene sandwiched between player portraits. *(Robert Edward Auctions LLC)*

Honus Wagner, the son of poor German immigrants, was one of the most beloved men in America. His celebrity made Andrew Carnegie so jealous that the industrialist turned philanthropist threatened to stop giving money to Pennsylvania communities unless fans started directing their love toward him. *(Courtesy of the Pittsburgh Pirates)*

The portrait that was used for the T206 Wagner was taken by photographer Carl Horner in his Boston studio in 1905. Horner was the premier baseball photographer of his day, and his work is featured prominently in the T206 set. The "Pittsburg" that is featured so prominently on the card wasn't in the original Wagner photo—it was added later by an artist. *(Robert Edward Auctions LLC)*

The Gretzky T206 Wagner is coveted by collectors not only because of its superb condition, but because its back features an advertisement for Piedmont cigarettes. Dozens of T206 Wagners still exist, but the vast majority feature ads for Sweet Caporals—only a few tout Piedmonts. *(Robert Edward Auctions LLC)*

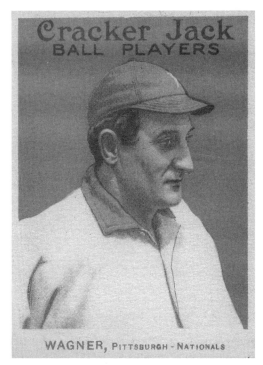

WAGNER, PITTSBURGH - NATIONALS

Honus Wagner was in the twilight of his career when his portrait appeared on this 1915 Cracker Jack card. The cards, inserted into boxes of the popcorn and caramel treat, are still popular with vintage collectors. *(Robert Edward Auctions LLC)*

The hobby's only uncut T206 proof strip was found in the attic of Honus Wagner's home in Carnegie, Pennsylvania, folded in the back pocket of his uniform pants. The strip might have been worth hundreds of thousands of dollars if it wasn't so badly creased. It sold for just $78,665 dollars in 2002. *(New York Daily News, L.P. Reprinted with permission.)*

This cigar band featuring "Hans" Wagner's likeness has been offered by some collectors as evidence that Wagner wasn't opposed to smoking. The Flying Dutchman did indeed enjoy cigars and chew tobacco. *(Robert Edward Auctions LLC)*

Honus Wagner's likeness was used to sell everything from cigars and beer to analgesic balm and gunpowder. Some companies paid him a token amount for his "endorsement." Others never bothered to ask for his consent. *(Robert Edward Auctions LLC)*

Rob Lifson, who lent Bill Mastro $25,000 to buy The Card in 1985, was just a kid when he started collecting and dealing vintage cards. He now runs Robert Edward Auctions, one of sports memorabilia's most prominent auction houses. *(Courtesy of Michael Gidwitz)*

Michael Gidwitz bought The Card for $640,000 in 1996 and sold it four years later for $1.27 million. In addition to baseball cards and sheets, he also collects original *MAD* magazine and Wacky Packages art. *(Courtesy of Michael Gidwitz)*

Bill Hughes was one of the Professional Sports Authenticator (PSA) graders who gave The Card its "PSA 8 NEAR MINT–MINT" mark. He is now a card and comic-book dealer who lives in Texas. *(Courtesy of Michael Gidwitz)*

Rob Lifson, Michael Gidwitz, and Bill Mastro were once close friends, but those days are long over. *(Courtesy of Michael Gidwitz)*

By 2001, Bill Mastro had turned Mastro Auctions into sports memorabilia's top auction house. Mastro has been involved as a buyer, seller, bidder, or auctioneer almost every time The Card has changed hands. *(Courtesy of Bridget Cicenia)*

This advertisement appeared in Wal-Mart stores to promote a contest called the "World's Most Valuable Trading Card Giveaway." The top prize—The Card—was won by a Florida postal worker named Patricia Gibbs. *(Courtesy of Anderson Press)*

Wayne Gretzky, the greatest player in NHL history, bought The Card with Los Angeles Kings owner Bruce McNall. The Great One sold the card after McNall was indicted on federal fraud charges. *(New York Daily News, L.P. Reprinted with permission.)*

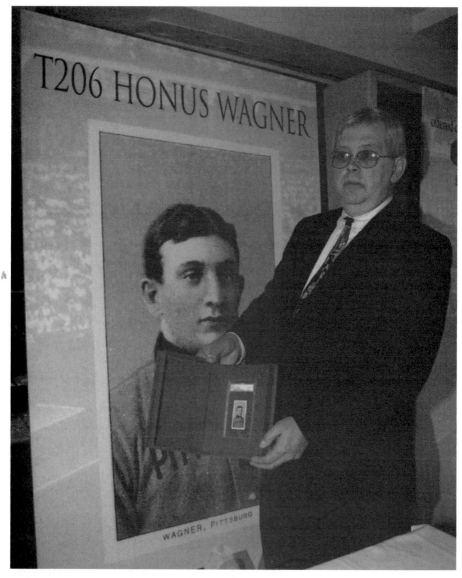

Mastro Auctions executive Don Flanagan shows off The Card during a 2000 press conference at Mickey Mantle's in New York City. The Card was purchased that summer by Southern California collector Brian Seigel for $1.27 million. *(New York Daily News, L.P. Reprinted with permission.)*

Ray Edwards, left, and John Cobb have waged a long and frustrating battle to prove their T206 Wagner is genuine. Many memorabilia collectors and dealers believe the Cincinnati men are trying to sell a counterfeit card, although paper and printing experts say it's possible the card is a hundred years old. *(Courtesy of Michael O'Keeffe)*

Honus Wagner has been largely forgotten in his hometown of Carnegie, Pennsylvania. One of the few reminders of baseball's greatest shortstop is the Honus Wagner Apartments for senior citizens and the disabled. *(Courtesy of Michael O'Keeffe)*

Carnegie residents saw Honus Wagner, seen here a few years before his death in 1955, as a good father, husband, and neighbor. Wagner loved to drink beer and tell tall tales at the Elks Club—when he wasn't playing ball with neighborhood kids. *(New York Daily News, L.P. Reprinted with permission.)*

Wagner lived in this house on Railroad Avenue in Carnegie until he was forty-two years old, when he married longtime girlfriend Bessie Smith. The home is now owned by Steelers fans with only fuzzy knowledge of Wagner's accomplishments. *(Courtesy of Michael O'Keeffe)*

Honus Wagner supervised construction of this home on Beechwood Avenue in Carnegie, where he and his wife, Bessie, raised their two daughters. Efforts to convert the pale brick home into a Wagner museum and bed-and-breakfast were shot down after neighbors expressed concerns about parking and other issues. *(Courtesy of Michael O'Keeffe)*

This statue of Honus Wagner, first erected at Schenley Park in 1955, was relocated to Pittsburgh's PNC Park. The inscription on the base calls Wagner "a champion among champions, whose record on and off the playing field of the national game will ever stand as a monument to his own greatness and as an example and inspiration to the youth of our country." *(Courtesy of Michael O'Keeffe)*

fattened primarily through baseball-card revenue—that could sustain its members through months of missed paychecks.

The following month acting commissioner Bud Selig canceled the rest of the season, including the playoffs. The World Series had endured for ninety years despite two world wars, the Depression, and the 1989 San Francisco earthquake, and fans were outraged that the Fall Classic had become a casualty to something many fans saw as a petty labor dispute between two greedy and arrogant factions. Several bills aimed at ending the strike were introduced into Congress, and President Clinton ordered both sides back to the bargaining table, giving them less than two weeks to reach a deal. His deadline came and went.

The 232-day strike did end in time for the 1995 season, but by then many Americans were fed up with baseball, and they turned their backs on the national pastime and everything associated with it. Major League Baseball attendance dropped to 50,469,236 in 1995, just a blip more than during the strike-shortened '94 season and well below the record 70,257,936 notched in 1993, the year the Colorado Rockies and Florida Marlins joined the National League. Sports-card sales crashed, too—annual sales dropped to $700 million in 1995—and drastic measures were still needed to keep the hobby from becoming a casualty of the most bitter labor battle in baseball history.

As the nation's largest retailer, Wal-Mart had a big stake in the shrinking card market: It sold far more baseball cards than did anyone else. Executives from Wal-Mart and Treat Entertainment knew they had to come up with something big, something spectacular that would grab fans' attention and draw them back to the hobby.

With support from Topps, Upper Deck, and other card companies, they came up with the aforementioned World's Most Valuable Card

Giveaway, a sweepstakes that ultimately drew more than a million entries. Treat Entertainment gave away rare and valuable cards as monthly prizes, including a 1980 Wayne Gretzky O-Pee-Chee card, a Topps Mickey Mantle rookie card, and a 1948 George Mikan rookie basketball card. A thousand entry cards, meanwhile, were selected at random each month as finalists for the grand prize, the Gretzky T206 Wagner.

To drum up publicity for the giveaway, Treat sent several traveling sports memorabilia "museums" to Wal-Mart stores across the country. The museums, special tractor-trailers that could be converted into gallery-style exhibitions in less than an hour by two "curators," would spend the day in the Wal-Mart parking lots in small towns and city suburbs, displaying rare old cards and game-used memorabilia such as a Mickey Mantle hat or a Hank Aaron glove. One of the traveling museums was called the "Wagner Museum," and it featured the trunk the Flying Dutchman used on road trips and a T206 Wagner owned by Treat chief executive officer Harold Anderson, an underbidder for The Card when McNall purchased it in 1991. Treat Entertainment also hired Baltimore Orioles Hall of Fame third baseman Brooks Robinson to accompany their Wagner Museum to Wal-Mart stores in Dallas, Chicago, Tampa, and other big cities.

"Brooks would fly in the day before," said John Appuhn, a spokesman for the company (which later changed its name to Anderson Press). "He'd go on the morning radio and TV shows, and in the afternoon he'd do interviews at the local newspapers. We were able to hit a lot of media that way."

The drawing for the grand prize was held on February 24, 1996—what would have been Honus Wagner's 122nd birthday—on CNN's *Larry King Weekend*. King had assembled an all-star panel for the show: Brooks Robinson, former Dodgers manager Tommy Lasorda, broadcaster Joe Garagiola, and a still-lanky Barry Bonds. The show was a typical King chatfest—the CNN star led the panel through a breezy conversation about the strike, the upcoming season, the fans, and baseball cards.

Finally the time came for the drawing—shortly after 9:00 P.M. Eastern time, Brooks Robinson cracked opened Honus Wagner's old steamer trunk. "I'll tell you, if I had to carry one of these, I wouldn't be ready to play," Robinson joked. "I'd be tired."

King stuck his arm inside the trunk, mixed up the four thousand entries, and pulled one out. "Okay, I picked one," he said. "This is the winner. I'm looking at the name. I am going to hand this to our control-room people. We're going to go back to the set and call the winner from our control room. We'll be right back with the winner of the $451,000 Honus Wagner card on *Larry King Weekend*. The trunk is closed. Don't go away."

After the commercial break, King's staff dialed the number on the winning entry. The phone rang. And rang. And rang.

"Hello. You have reached the message center for Gonzalez . . ."

"Oh, that's the wrong name. It's wrong. We dialed the wrong number!" King spit out. "I'll announce the winner, and if you're there, please pick up the phone or correct the number. And the winner is . . . Patricia Gibbs . . . Hollywood, Florida. We'll attempt to reconnect to that number. We congratulate Patricia Gibbs. She wins this Honus Wagner $451,000 card (the amount Gretzky and McNall had paid for the card). We'll attempt to recontact her at the correct number. And we hope— Patricia, if you're watching, don't [tie up] the phone. This is yours, Patricia. This is worth a lot."

Later attempts to reach Gibbs were equally frustrating. "We have attempted again to try to reach Patricia Gibbs," King said later in the show. "We're getting that same answering machine, so, Patricia, if you are watching, or any friend of Patricia's is watching, the folks at Treat Entertainment will be in direct touch with you and you will get this card.

Gibbs, a forty-one-year-old postal clerk, wasn't watching. She didn't even have cable television. She finally did get a phone call late that night notifying her that she'd won; for the first time in a decade, The Card didn't belong to an obsessive collector or a rich man who wanted to flaunt his wealth. It belonged to a regular person.

"I feel like I won the lottery," Gibbs said. "I couldn't believe it."

Treat and Wal-Mart executives awarded the Gretzky T206 Wagner to Gibbs a few weeks later at the Miramar, Florida, Wal-Mart store—the same nondescript store where she'd entered the contest. Gibbs, accompanied by her family, told reporters she would consign The Card to an auction later that year. She couldn't afford the taxes on a $451,000 sweepstakes prize, and she could use the money when she retired from the postal service in a few years.

Gibbs said she didn't know much about Wagner before the drawing. "But now it's like I know him personally," she said.

Gibbs was deluged with calls from auction houses who wanted the publicity and the commission that would come with selling the most famous baseball card in the world. Christie's, the 230-year-old auction house better known for selling van Goghs, Rembrandts, and Picassos, took a different tack: Christie's executive Mary Hoeveler got in line at the Ocean View post office, where Gibbs worked as a clerk, and made her pitch. The personal approach worked. Gibbs agreed to sell the card at Christie's.

The promotion was a big success for Treat Entertainment and Wal-Mart. Over the course of the four months, they sold 30 million packs of cards, 418 percent more than before the promotion. They had reversed the sharp declines in sales. Unfortunately for the world of cards, that reversal wouldn't stick.

The old Fort Washington Expo Center outside Philadelphia was the site of many card shows before a real estate development company purchased the former Honeywell International factory and announced in January 2006 that it planned to convert the 290,000-square-foot building into an office complex. The center, surrounded by business-park edifices and acres of parking lots, is a squat structure with all the flair of a cinder block. Still, many collectors will always have a place in their hearts for the center. For more than a decade, hobby insiders had spent several weekends a year under its flickering fluorescent lights, breathing its stale air and eating cold hot dogs, buying and selling cards, and swapping stories.

The news spread like a prairie fire at the March 2006 show, and the old expo center's impending closure made the show feel like a party that had ended hours earlier, the champagne gone flat, the dip curdled. Regional shows like Fort Washington tend to draw much smaller crowds than the National, comprising primarily serious collectors looking to fill holes in their collections. Few of the attendees showed any delight in being there, and many had that glazed-over *Night of the Living Dead* look. They gathered around the hot-dog stands and in the makeshift cafeteria to discuss the show's offerings, then retreated to the parking lot, which was filled with SUVs and pickup trucks, mostly there for the RV show in the adjacent building. The license plates that once would have reflected the distance card collectors would travel to find a show now spoke of the geographical diversity of those looking for mobile homes.

There were few kids and very few casual browsers. This was an all-business crowd, mostly men in their forties and fifties wearing the remaining vestiges of their youth—graying ponytails, old base-ball caps, rock T-shirts stretched across ample midsections. Some were accompanied by wives or children, but most strolled alone or in small groups past tables loaded with cards, autographed photos, bobbleheads, old newspaper clippings. The last people obsessed with trading cards, it seemed, grew up in the 1950s, '60s, and '70s. Following generations have forgotten about the joys of trading cards and have found other things—video games and MySpace.com—to entertain them.

The hobby, it appears, is in critical condition. There will un-doubtedly always be a hard-core base of card collectors, but the boom days are long gone, maybe forever. The hobby peaked in 1991, when McNall and Gretzky made international headlines by purchasing their T206 Wagner and fans bought $1.2 billion worth of new cards, but it has been in free fall ever since.

By 2005, annual sales of new trading cards had dropped more than 75 percent to about $250 million a year. Other indicators are equally bleak: The number of card shops in the United States, for example, has plummeted from ten thousand to roughly seventeen hundred. Many of those shop owners undoubtedly took their busi-ness to the Internet—why pay retail clerks and rent a store in a shop-ping mall if you can do all your business online? Many others, however, took a beating.

Attendance at the July 2006 National Sports Collectors Conven-tion in Anaheim, California, meanwhile, was thirty-five thousand over four days, a fraction of the one hundred thousand plus who jammed into the Anaheim Convention Center in 1991, forcing the fire marshal to close the show doors. Still, the crowd was much live-lier than the moribund bunch at the Fort Washington show a few months earlier—kids dashed excitedly from booth to booth while huge crowds lined up to pay as much as $200 for autographs from retired A-list athletes such as Joe Montana, Troy Aikman, Dave Winfield, and Rod Carew and current stars such as Reggie Bush and Matt Leinart.

Some dealers complained that the convention center seemed half empty and that business was down. Southern California is not the strongest market for sports collectibles—the hobby's roots run deepest in the Midwest and the Northeast—but the sagging attendance at the 2006 National seemed indicative of bigger problems. At the height of the baseball-card gold fever, regional shows were held in major cities at least once a month. But as interest in cards waned, so did attendance at card shows, and by 2005 most cities could only host shows once every two or three months.

Baseball-card manufacturers, meanwhile, are in disarray. Fleer declared bankruptcy in 2005. In July 2006, as Topps' promotions staff was drawing huge crowds to its display at the National with free cards and Bazooka gum, its top executives were battling back a coup by dissident investors who were angry about declining card sales, stagnant stock prices, and what they called excessive executive compensation and calcified corporate leadership. Upper Deck, which purchased Fleer's assets, didn't seem bruised by the declining market, but that's because the company had long ago diversified into autographed sports memorabilia, trading-card games, and other areas.

Donruss, meanwhile, had been pushed out of the baseball-card business by the Major League Baseball Players Association, which in late 2005 cut back the number of licensees to two—Topps and Upper Deck. The number of card sets was slashed from eighty-nine in 2004 to forty, and the union put $3 million into a marketing campaign to teach kids how to play with trading cards. Topps and Upper Deck launched their own marketing efforts, too.

None of that was very comforting to Mike Berkus, the co-executive director of the National and an important figure in the hobby since 1970.

"I don't believe we ever had to do a marketing campaign to get people to buy trading cards. For ten-year-olds, the passion for collecting doesn't come from somebody telling you how to do it," Berkus said as he relaxed in an Anaheim Convention Center conference room during the 2006 National. "Card collecting is a passion. You either love 'em or you don't."

THE COLLECTOR

In the fall of 1996, Michael Gidwitz was focused on the Gretzky T206 and was determined to own it. It's one thing to meticulously amass a collection of vintage *Mad* magazine art and vintage paintings and rare baseball cards worth millions, but it's another to possess the Mona Lisa and all the attention that comes with it. As one East Coast collector says, "Some people get into the hobby because they need approval. They think they are important people because they own a Joe DiMaggio bat or a T206 Wagner. They need to own the very best."

Gidwitz, a stocky man whose sandy hair wisps across his forehead and who keeps a Bentley in the garage of his Chicago condominium building, himself seems to understand this.

"I don't care if I have the biggest collection. I don't care if I have the best collection," he said. "I care about how much fun I have."

But the fifty-six-year-old Gidwitz is also a shrewd businessman, and he recognized the value of what Mastro was creating in the Gretzky T206 Wagner almost from the start: He loathes Mastro now, and what he has done to the collectibles industry, but Gidwitz himself profited off Mastro's machinations with The Card, and not only financially. Like the addict who craves the ultimate fix, Gidwitz knew that his card collection was missing something: the pure hit that would provide that euphoric high. In 1996 the Gretzky T206 was just about the best drug he could get his hands on. Gidwitz had already bid $300,000 on The Card at the Copeland Auction in 1991 and had been thwarted by what he felt was another setup by Mastro, who was running the auction for Sotheby's.

Gidwitz knew on that March day in 1991 that The Card had become the symbol of an exploding industry, and that by 1996 it had taken on its own legend beyond the depiction of a turn-of-the-century shortstop with parted black hair and rosy cheeks. It had become a media event, a symbol of a hobby that was now making headlines. Suddenly there was an audience eager to look behind the glass cases and the dusty catalogs of serious collectors. Suddenly its mysterious history was enhanced.

Gidwitz had been telling people he was going to try to buy The Card again at the Christie's auction in '96, and he enlisted his long-time pal Rob Lifson to bid on it. Gidwitz sat next to Lifson during the bidding in the stately, regal room in the venerable East Side auction house, but he never raised his own hand, never even held a paddle. It added to the mystery—and the thrill of the chase. Only the insiders knew, for instance, that the bidding process itself was tilted in Gidwitz's favor, much as Gidwitz felt it had been tilted to Gretzky five years earlier at Sotheby's, when Mastro was virtually controlling the bidding over the telephone. People at Christie's are fond of Gidwitz—he is affable and always respectful—and it paid off that day.

"It pays to be nice to people," Gidwitz would say later. "If I was the guy bidding against you, when you bid, they go real slow; when I bid, they go real fast."

In other words, the auctioneers wouldn't give the other bidders as much time. Some people complained about it, but whom were they really going to complain to? The auction houses are as complicit in the backroom deals as the dealers and collectors and authenticators: They provide their high rollers with hotel suites—they often put Gidwitz up in a plush apartment at the old Hotel Delmonico on Park Avenue, with flowers and wine. Some of the women who work at Christie's are Gidwitz's close friends, he said. In fact, the night before the auction, one of the Christie's executives had taken him out to dinner and warned him that a corporation was planning to get the Wagner.

"You better be willing to spend a million dollars," she told him.

After the bidding reached $550,000, it inexpicably slowed. Mastro was still in, as was Richard Gelman, the son of Topps baseball-card artist Woody Gelman. But when Lifson raised his hand at $580,000, the others dropped out. Despite his claim that he would bid on The Card, Gidwitz had kept his intentions fairly quiet, and even during the auction it was unclear that he'd bought it.

When he gave the high sign to Lifson and the hammer came down, Lifson was easily as happy as Gidwitz.

"He was so ecstatic, he was just going crazy," Gidwitz said. Gidwitz had a letter from his bank proving he had a line of credit for $1 million and that he was authorized to use it. He'd been prepared to spend up to $800,000; he felt he'd gotten a bargain at $641,500, including buyer's premium.

And suddenly Mike Gidwitz was the slightly mysterious owner of the Gretzky T206, the best baseball card money could buy.

"I think The Card was a better buy at $640,000 than it was at $451,000, because if I had bought the card for $451,000, it wouldn't have gotten the notoriety that it got when Gretzky and McNall bought it," Gidwitz would say. "That gave it some kind of history, a story, it added to the legend for this card. It added to the prestige of it."

Gidwitz was convinced that The Card would eventually sell for $1 million, and he wanted to be the first collector to get that price for a baseball card. To make that kind of decision, you have to be prepared for the risk, and Gidwitz was.

"I knew that I would never be under duress to sell The Card. That I would never be forced to sell it. That I could keep it for the rest of my life if I wanted to. Because it wasn't going to alter my life. And some day that card will sell for a million bucks if I feel like selling it. Today I would sell it, tomorrow I might not," he said just after he bought The Card.

"You know, your feelings about things change. If someone offered me $1 million for it today, I'd really have to think about it. But today I'd be able to enjoy the fact that I did something right, that I'd made 56 percent return on my money after the carrying costs. And that I'd be the only person in the world ever to sell a baseball card for a million bucks. I mean, that's gotta be a kick! Still, no matter what happens, nobody can take away the fact that I owned this card, even if it's only for a little while."

After he bought The Card at the Christie's auction, Gidwitz brought it to Lifson's house in suburban New Jersey, where he and Lifson took photos of themselves with it. During the four years he owned it, he kept it in his apartment for about two months before it went to one of his safe-deposit boxes in a downtown Chicago bank.

Of course, carrying around the Gretzky T206 in your wallet is never going to do, and even in his delirious happiness over getting The Card, Gidwitz knew he would never really be able to show it off to the friends and visitors who would come to his home, or even hang it on the wall or set it on his coffee table. He'd been victimized by thieves—not thugs with guns drawn, mind you, but respectable businessmen, even friends and acquaintances—too many times to think otherwise.

Gidwitz owns the entire floor of one of the postmodern apartment buildings that line Lake Shore Drive, not looming over Lake Michigan so much as melding seamlessly into the horizon as you gaze out the big windows of the apartment. Inside, it's a different story.

On one wall of his sparsely furnished living room hangs a painting of the T206 Wagner—except instead of Wagner the painting depicts, as do most of the drawings and paintings in Gidwitz's unique art collection, a misbehaving Alfred E. Neuman. The Gretzky T206 Wagner had brought Gidwitz fame and acclaim, but that was ages ago, and Gidwitz is now focused mostly on his strange collection of original art. Neuman is clearly Gidwitz's alter ego. In one painting a Snow White figure is surrounded by the seven dwarves with Neumanesque faces—one is humping Snow White's leg, another is lighting small animals on fire with a blowtorch, another hangs from a chandelier. A Neuman statue sits on an end table. In the corner stands an eight-foot-tall replica the of the monster that terrorized Sigourney Weaver in *Alien*, a massive grayish green lizard hovering over the large room.

But it is the adjoining apartment that defines the mind-set of a wealthy collector. In the drawers and cubbyholes of the extra apartment, tucked away in the locked boxes and packed in stuffed, bulging closets, rest the objects of Gidwitz's obsessions—ancient baseball-card collections, pristine sheets of old cards that look fresh off the printing press, a Norman Rockwell parody here and there, and, of course, interpretations of Neuman painted by the same artists who actually drew the *Mad* magazine covers they mimic. Gidwitz hires the artists, then instructs them to impose his image on Neuman. Some are silly. Some are intriguing. Many are pornographic. All are viewed by their owner with a kind of adolescent wonder. There is no furniture to speak of in the apartment, no sign that anyone other than the ghosts of old baseball players and an imaginary character from a satiric magazine live there.

"Isn't this great?" he asks, pulling from a drawer a rendition of Bill Clinton and Monica Lewinsky leaning over Neuman's superimposed mug on the former president's penis head. "Don't you love this? It's really bad, isn't it?"

His family is renowned for its art collection, but to Gidwitz his odd assortment of collectibles is more meaningful, his Rockwell parodies more valuable than originals. "I'd rather have my stuff than the originals, because I enjoy them more," he said.

The *Chicago Sun-Times* once described the separate apartment as "what has to be Chicago's most unusual condominium."

That may be an understatement. In the late nineties, the *Sun-Times* estimated Gidwitz's collection to be worth between $10 million and $20 million, but it would surely bring more in today's inflated collectibles market. He has drawers of uncut sheets, many one-of-a-kind, pristine works of art that are worth millions on their own, including a complete Goudey set from 1933 that is the only uncut set of its kind, and boxes of rare cards. There's a 1960 Topps set here, another Goudey there, a T206 collection in that corner, a gorgeous Mickey Mantle under that pile.

Gidwitz isn't even sure of what he has in the battered old shoe boxes and dusty corners of the apartment. But his face reddens and his voice rises as he pulls out the original paintings used by the card companies to create many of the cards in his collection. Some members of Gidwitz's family recently sold a Picasso for $95.2 million, the second-highest price ever paid for a work of art, to a mysterious bidder in an auction at Sotheby's, but the art in this apartment is as stunning in its own way as any painting hanging in a museum. These sheets and paintings are the "precious papers" of Gidwitz's collection ("Preciouspaper" is the name of Gidwitz's Web site), the truly rare—and, more important to him—authentic pieces, the only things left in the hobby worth acquiring.

Gidwitz is getting out of the card business—"I love the cards, but things have changed," he says—and he is moving on.

Even now, when you walk into Gidwitz's apartment, the walls are mostly bare, the tables unadorned. He says it is because the apartment is being painted and recarpeted, but the real reason is that people lift things from Gidwitz: Wacky Packs, baseball cards, matchbooks, ashtrays, some valuable, some worthless. Problem is, when you're a collector like Gidwitz, people assume that everything you have is valuable. And most things are: Someone once stole—from Gidwitz's house—a couple of Ruth cards from his Goudey Gum Company set, reducing its value from $100,000 to $40,000.

"You know, they always want to see my set," he said. "I spent thirty years putting that set together, upgrading the cards. It changed, it took something away. You feel raped, you feel violated. You don't feel the same. I trusted people, everybody who came into my house. I don't know what happened, maybe I went to the bathroom."

Gidwitz once caught a visitor pocketing a card that he was preparing to sell.

"I had spent about $750 on this card," he said, "and it was worth maybe about $500. These two people came—an adult and a kid—and suddenly the card wasn't there. I said, 'I want to see your pocket, and the guy said, 'I don't want you to do that.' I know it is in his pocket.

I told him that I would let him have the card that he just bought for free, but not if you have that card in your pocket. There was a tussle, and I knocked the guy across the fucking table, and I took the card out of his pocket and told him to leave. Right in front of the kid. I broke my fucking hand."

Unlike some collectibles, such as the Edvard Munch painting *The Scream*, which was heisted in August 2003 in full view of patrons at Oslo's Munch Museum and wasn't found for three years, or any of the massively valuable works of art that find a market in underground dealing and collecting, it is difficult to hide extremely rare cards such as T206 Wagners. Conversely, it is virtually impossible to identify more common stolen items on the market. How do you tell one Mickey Mantle from another? How do you know which one is yours?

So Gidwitz took out a massive insurance policy on the Gretzky T206 and had it delivered to his home by Brink's. When he had guests over, Gidwitz would surreptitiously go into this closet to look at it, kind of like a fourteen-year-old boy sneaking a peek at his *Playboy*.

Gidwitz grew up across the street from the Drake Hotel in Chicago, the grandson of the founder of Lanzit Corrugated Box Company (his uncle, Gerald, who died in June 2006 at age ninety-nine, founded the Helene Curtis cosmetics company). He attended the Lawrenceville School, a prep school in New Jersey, and the University of Arizona, where he studied English and creative writing. He says he once wrote comedy material for Sam Kinison. He doesn't have a laptop and rarely uses a cell phone.

Gidwitz began collecting baseball cards when he was about eight, the same age as many boys who amassed collections and then somehow lost them. He first collected cards with his brother Jimmy as a kid, and then Gidwitz turned them into arguably the best baseball-card collection in the world.

Now Gidwitz and Jimmy are at odds over the cards. It's a dicey issue.

"I remember my father telling me not to collect together, because we would both be unhappy, and if you're not both unhappy, then one of you is going to be really unhappy, and I think it's going to be you, because you're spending a lot of money on this," Gidwitz said.

Gidwitz hopes they can sort it out peacefully, just like they did when they were boys.

"Our dad was busy, he didn't have a lot of time," Gidwitz said. "So I played with my brother. We played ball—and we would divide up the draft, like maybe I would have the National League and he would have the American League, and you get the first pick and I get the second pick, or we would work something out like that. We would trade the cards—just like fantasy football. He was six and a half years older than me, so he was ahead of me—he started collecting in '52. The first pack I bought was a 1958 Topps pack. The first card was a Harmon Killebrew with a yellow background."

When Gidwitz talks about the Wagner, he does so with a kind of wistfulness—it was a great card to own, he had fun owning it, but once the reporters stopped calling and casual acquaintances stopped asking about it, he began to lose interest in it. Collectors of baseball cards are like other collectors—they often move from one obsession to the next. And Gidwitz was discovering something else: The card-collecting hobby was not all it should be. Things were going on that he couldn't justify. It's one thing to spend hundreds of thousands of dollars on a card that you know has been trimmed; it's another to sell altered, fraudulent items to unsuspecting customers. Whatever innocence had surrounded it in the halcyon days of his childhood was being lost.

The questions put to Gidwitz in the aftermath of his purchase never really went much beyond the obvious: Why is The Card so valuable? What is it about The Card that you find so attractive? What will you do with it? Will you sell it? Why the Honus Wagner? Gidwitz gave the usual answers. "Well, I always wanted a nice one. I didn't want a beat-up one," he said.

When asked where it had been all those years before Mastro bought it and how it was that it was in such good shape, he was vague.

"I don't know," he said. "I thought it was in a desk. I can't say."

But while Gidwtiz did reveal something in those early interviews about his motives for buying the card—he said he wanted to be the first person to sell a baseball card for $1 million—until recently he never discussed the actual shape the Gretzky T206 was in, whether it was altered in some way, whether it was truly a pristine, priceless piece of history.

Now he says flatly that he bought the card "as is." He had looked at it in the 1991 Copeland sale and decided it met his criteria for excellence—it was just the best Wagner out there.

"I looked at the card, and I'm not saying it wasn't cut off a sheet. I'm not saying it was trimmed or not, and I don't care. I just didn't want any mangled cards, no creased cards," he says now. "I never owned any creased cards in my personal collection. I don't want trimmed cards either, but I did want a Wagner card."

So whatever had been done to get The Card into its current shape really didn't seem to matter to Gidwitz. He does not have his cards graded, doesn't trust the process, doesn't see the value. And he knows that just surviving the roiling waters of the purchasing process is where the real negotiating is done, where the real value is set. Gidwitz had tried to buy another Wagner from Lelands owner Josh Evans years before he bought the Gretzky Wagner but lost out when Evans decided to auction The Card. "He wanted the prestige of auctioning it," said Gidwitz, who'd offered $100,000 for that card. "They know in advance whether or not they are going to fuck you. I wanted to put up the first bid of $100,000 when they auctioned it, and Josh wouldn't let me put up the bid. He let Bill bid."

Gidwitz may seem quirky, but he is a sophisticated collector. Gidwitz knew all the rumors about The Card's flaws and, based on his experience as a collector, suspected it had been trimmed. "It never came up," insists Lifson, of whether Gidwitz would have even cared. "It just didn't matter."

For Gidwitz himself this presents something of a conundrum. He has profited from a card he believes is trimmed—yet he detests the hucksters and grifters who have invaded the hobby. It is why he no longer collects baseball cards.

"Unfortunately," he said, "as time progressed, cards became more valuable, so unscrupulous people learned how to fix them. That was part of the reason I decided to stop collecting baseball cards."

Gidwitz and other superior collectors now prefer to acquire sheets of uncut cards—they are presumed to be the only "pure" cards left on the market. Gidwitz said the issue of trust is at the heart of the problems that plague the industry. How, for instance, can you be sure that the card you send in to have graded is the same one that is sent back to you?

"Do you even remember the condition your card was in? What

keeps the grading companies from juicing the grade, especially to their valued customers? Let's say you have your cards graded, and your cards all come out eights, sevens, and sixes. Let's say that one of those big auction houses has them graded, and they know how to take creases out, they know how to work with corners," he said. "Card guys that they hire, they hire away from the grading services. They are experts. Somebody who is sending in a thousand cards a week says, 'Can you give this card a little something extra? It's a six, and I want it to be a seven. Will you do that for me? Otherwise I'm going to go to the other company.' There are just too many problems with cards. That's why I collect artwork—and sheets."

He thinks he can spot reprints, but he isn't always sure, not with the laser printers forgers use today.

"Look, there are too many problems," Gidwitz said. "It turned me off after a while, you know. You just say, 'Fuck it.'"

Once it became clear to Gidwitz that he could indeed get over $1 million for The Card, there was really no choice but to get rid of it. Gidwitz began seriously thinking about selling the Gretzky T206 after the now-legendary Halper auction of 1999, during which actor Billy Crystal famously paid $239,000 for a circa-1960 Mickey Mantle glove that was later proved to have been used toward the end of Mantle's career. Gidwitz and Lifson were at the auction and saw Crystal buy the glove. Gidwitz immediately turned to his friend and said, "You know when a guy has too much money and he doesn't have time to spend it? Well, I think it is a really good time for me to sell the Wagner and get a million dollars." "You know what?" Lifson responded. "That might be a good idea."

On July 15, 2000, Gidwitz and Lifson sold the PSA NM-MT 8 Wagner T206 through a sale on eBay to a California collector named

Brian Seigel for $1.265 million, the highest price ever paid for a baseball card. Gidwitz had gotten his million-dollar price. He was happy enough that Seigel got the card, although he is unhappy even now that Mastro is usually referenced in media reports as having arranged the sale.

"I want to make it clear," he said. "Do you understand? It really fucking irritates me. I want to make it perfectly clear who sold the Honus Wagner card. It was me and Rob."

Gidwitz got one more day in the sun. All the trips to the grocery store to buy a new pack of cards, the trades in the schoolyards, the wheeling and dealing in the auction houses, the thefts, the disappointments, all fell away on the day he sold the Gretzky T206.

"I had the opportunity to have the best available card," he said. "I was the top guy on the hill. That benchmark—I'll always be part of the story. I just know that of all the guys that owned the Wagner, I had the most fun."

Gidwitz still talks about the cards as if it all happened yesterday. He remembers the feel of the cards, the autumn days, the boys themselves. "Collecting has been going on since the beginning of time," he said. "My mother collected antiques. When I was in the first grade, I traded for a Dale Long card. I must've given the guy ten or twelve cards that he needed. Scott Schissler was the kid's name. It's important to remember people."

His voice drifts off as he thinks about his brother—and the unpleasantness that sometimes now surrounds their relationship, all because of the cards. But he isn't going to let himself get caught up in the money, won't let it ruin his memories of their childhood or the lessons he learned at the kitchen table, the cards spread out before them like the loot from a bank heist.

"I remember having a Gil Hodges from 1959, me and my brother. We always tried to have two of everything, but we only had one of that one. If there are cards on the table, you can't have anything that would potentially damage them. I always drink Cokes in the kitchen. I knocked over a Coke, and it stained the Hodges, and I never got another one."

In many ways his situation with his brother is just a chapter in the bigger story and the fight to expose the corruption, to shine a light on what was in Gidwitz's mind the pure pursuit of the past. But no matter what happens to the hobby, Gidwitz got the Mona Lisa. Over and over, as he hurries through his apartments looking for the pristine sheets, and the stickers with his own crazy designs painted on them, and the Wacky Packs, and the original paintings, and the gorgeous baseball cards, he always returns to the Wagner.

"See," he said, "the Wagner is overwhelmingly considered to be the best card. And I increased the story. I enhanced its value. I took it over a certain hurdle. I broke the four-minute mile."

AIN'T NOTHIN' LIKE THE REAL THING

If card shop owners had a dollar for every time someone came into their shop and said he'd be rich if only his mother hadn't thrown out his baseball cards, every card shop in America would be closed: The owners would be Bill Gates wealthy, and they would have long ago retired to their own private tropical islands. The whining over lost cards is a condition that afflicts even the most powerful. When President George W. Bush was a kid, he would send big leaguers their cards, along with self-addressed envelopes, hoping they would autograph the cards and mail them back. Bush says he had a massive collection during the 1950s and '60s, but they mysteriously disappeared.

"He's still mad at me," an exasperated Barbara Bush once said of the forty-third president of the United States. "He thinks I threw away his baseball cards. 'They'd be worth millions now.' I'm quoting him: 'Millions now.'"

Of course, it wouldn't be much of a hobby if mothers hadn't thrown out baseball cards. Old cards are valuable because they were made to be disposable. So there is at least some irony in the fact that the finest museums in the world include baseball cards—flimsy pieces of cardboard whose original purpose was to sell tobacco or candy—in their collections. To museum curators and art historians, baseball cards are interesting because of what they represent: a printing technique, a time period. Museums include cards in their collections because they illustrate baseball's importance in American life for more than a century and because they demonstrate advances in printing technology, advertising, and marketing.

The Department of Drawings and Prints at New York City's Metropolitan Museum of Art has a T206 Wagner that would drive many collectors crazy with desire. The card has what collectors would call an outstanding lineage: It was one of the three hundred thousand plus cards donated to the museum in 1947 by Jefferson Burdick, the Syracuse factory worker known as the father of card collecting, thanks to the systems he developed to organize and catalog trading cards. Although the card at the Met looks worn compared to the Gretzky T206 Wagner—it has dirty edges and dog-eared corners—it has no apparent creasing, holes, or tears and would sell for at least $100,000 and probably far more if it were consigned to Mastro Auctions or another sports-memorabilia house.

At the Met the card is rarely displayed for the public—it is occasionally removed from a museum storage room. When it is on display, visitors have to make an appointment to see it. It was taped into a light brown frame years ago, and the current Drawings and Prints Department staff no longer even knows what brand of cigarettes is featured on the back. The white matting around the T206 makes the thin slice of cardboard seem even more insignificant.

"Nobody here would argue that it is great art like a Rembrandt or a Picasso," said George Goldner, the chairman of the department. "It is not great art. We don't pretend that it is. It was accepted because it was part of the printed imagery of the West."

Card collectors can take comfort in the fact that Goldner said the

Metropolitan Museum of Art's T206 Wagner is "a perfectly nice-looking image." That's much nicer than the assessment offered by a Met curatorial assistant in a 1990 interview. "I thought baseball cards were put in spokes, not museums," Tom Rassieur told *The New Yorker*, annoyed that the card was taking up any space at all in the museum.

The New York Public Library's T206 Wagner is kept in a big blue album with other T206 cards that can be viewed in the Brooke Russell Astor Reading Room for Rare Books and Manuscripts, a dark, scholarly room full of heavy wooden tables and lined with shelves full of leather-bound books.

The card, part of the thousand-card collection donated by a collector named Leopold Morse Goulston in 1946, is in pretty bad shape. The edges are filthy, the corners are floppy, and the borders are unevenly cut. The card was glued onto the page fifty years ago, and the back would probably be severely damaged if someone tried to remove it. Visitors rarely ask to see the Wagner T206, and the library staff doesn't regard it as anything special, although a special pass is required to get into the Brooke Russell Astor Reading Room. Security is always a concern.

"They're little," curator Virginia Bartow says of T206 cards. "It's easy to slip one in a shirt pocket. It only takes one person."

Compare the Met's and the NYPL's nonchalance with this flowery entry in a 2005 Mastro Auctions catalog, which makes a T206 Wagner that sold for $236,000 sound like a cross between an opiate and a religious icon: "The mere sight of a T206 Wagner is sufficient to provoke an unbelievably pleasant sensation, unique to each individual, within the emotional core of a baseball enthusiast," the catalog copy said, describing a card that was given a mere two on PSA's one-to-ten grading scale.

"Here is the item that has inspired the industry from its earliest days, and the artifact that continues to be the ultimate goal for every enthusiast. Honus Wagner's presence elevates any collection like no other force on the planet, but so lamentably few of the industry's finest assemblies have the opportunity to attain the resultant, ultra-elite status thus afforded."

Mastro's copywriter would find a kindred spirit in Edward Wharton Tigar, the English spymaster who donated his one-million-card collection to London's British Museum. Tigar had already staked out his place in history during World War II—he was responsible for blowing up a German monitoring station that had threatened Allied landings in North Africa. Later, in China, he operated the biggest black-market-currency operation in history. But Tigar's pride and joy was his tobacco-card collector, which has found a home at the museum alongside the Elgin Marbles, the Rosetta Stone, and other antiquities from ancient Rome, Greece, Egypt, and Mesopotamia. After the war Tigar became a mining mogul, and one benefit of his business travels was the opportunity to add to his card collection. When his home literally overflowed with cards, he bought the house next door and, much like Michael Gidwitz in Chicago, filled that up, too.

"I fully recognized that there are those who think, and will always think, that people must be very odd to devote time, effort and money to the collection of such things as stamps, matchbox labels and cigarette cards," Tigar wrote in his autobiography. "For me, my collection has not only afforded countless hours of pleasure, but in a busy business career it provided a diversion and relaxation in times of stress. . . . If to collect cigarette cards is a sign of eccentricity, how then will posterity judge one who amassed the biggest collection in the world? Frankly, I care not."

The Baseball Hall of Fame has two T206 Wagners. One remains on permanent display in Cooperstown; the other is part of the Hall's traveling exhibition that has toured the country in recent years. Both came from the famed Barry Halper collection. Halper donated one of the cards to the Hall during the 1980s. The other Wagner is the card Bill Mastro gave Rob Lifson back in 1985—the one Lifson sold to Halper for $30,000—to repay the $25,000 loan used to purchase what eventually became the Gretzky T206 Wagner. In 1999, Major League Baseball spent $5 million to purchase that card and other artifacts from Halper and donated them to Cooperstown. One high-end collector who owns a T206 Wagner and preferred to conduct his business in anonymity said the only Wagner card he would be interested in trading his own card for is the one in the Hall of Fame. There are too many rumors surrounding the others, including the Gretzky T206. "If I'm buying a card," the collector said, "I don't care what the grading company said. If I don't feel a card is good, I'm not buying it."

The Hall of Fame is hallowed ground for those who believe that baseball is more religion than sport, but in Cooperstown the cards are regarded more as interesting curios than as religious icons. Curator Ted Spencer smirked when asked if the Hall would ever consider getting its T206 Wagners graded.

"That's for those *other* people," Spencer said, barely restraining his disdain for card fetishists. "These are historic artifacts. We don't care if the corners are rounded or straight. They are in our collection because baseball cards have been important in our culture since the 1880s."

LOST AND FOUND

Some longtime collectors and dealers believe that there are fewer than forty T206 Wagner cards still around. Others estimate there may be as many as a hundred or more. Nobody doubts that there are at least a handful of T206 Wagners still undiscovered, stashed in long-forgotten family Bibles and photo albums.

The odds might be greater than hitting the lottery, but it does happen. In 2001 a Philadelphia family found a box containing more than twenty-five hundred cards in their attic, including a T206 Wagner. Even more remarkable, the card had the rare Piedmont back. Although it was in poor condition, it sold a few months later at a Mastro auction for more than $86,000. The cards, undisturbed for thirty years, also came with a 1958 letter offering the consignor's father $25 for the Wagner.

"This sounded fascinating, but unfortunately the family did not think this letter was significant and did not know where they put it," Mastro's Web site reported. "Our guess and our hope was that perhaps the letter was from Charles Bray, the first full-time baseball card dealer. Bray ran the first auction devoted to card collecting in the world. Anyone who was serious about collecting older cards from the 1930s well into the 1960s bought and sold cards through Bray's Card Collectors

Bulletin. Aside from Bray, there really weren't many dealers in rare vintage cards in the 1950s. Our excitement about the letter resulted in a frantic and thorough search—and the letter was finally found. It was, indeed, from the legendary Charles Bray."

The original envelope—postmarked April 17, 1958—and advertising flyers for *The American Card Catalog* and the *Card Collectors Bulletin* accompanied the letter.

"To most hobby scholars," Mastro's Web site added, "this letter adds an additional unique dimension to this already very significant Wagner, and contributes to making this card stand out all the more from the pack as one of the most significant and noteworthy of all T206 Wagners."

In 2002, meanwhile, a man who had just recently moved to the United States from Europe found 350 T206 cards, some T205 cards, and felt pennants in an antique trunk in the attic of a Florida home he was refurbishing. There were no Wagners in the trunk, according to *Sports Collectors Digest.* But the cache did include a Ty Cobb, a Nap Lajoie, a rare Sherry Magee, and a couple of Cy Youngs and Christy Mathewsons, as well as many other Hall of Famers and hard-to-find minor leaguers. Usually, however, people who think they hit the jackpot wind up disappointed. Longtime dealer Al "Mr. Mint" Rosen says he's often approached at card shows by people who believe they've found a T206 Wagner in a deceased grandfather's footlocker or an uncle's sock drawer. Rosen says it's no fun being the guy who has to break the bad news.

"There are thousands of reproductions out there," Mr. Mint says. "I can tell across the room, in less than a second, that they are no good."

Most of those people, Rosen believes, aren't trying to pull a fast one. They truly believe they have the real McCoy, he says, and it's hard to fault them for hoping they beat the odds and got lucky. In recent years the price of a T206 Wagner has appreciated faster than Manhattan real estate. In September 2000, for example, a Wagner T206 graded a two on PSA's one-to-ten scale sold for $75,000. Five years later another PSA 2 T206 Wagner sold for more than three times that amount—a whopping $237,000. At the same auction, a PSA 1 Wagner sold for $110,000. In 2005, Mastro Auctions sold a T206 owned by Bill Mastro's mentor, Frank Nagy, for $456,000.

Even bureaucrats have caught T206 gold fever. In 2000, West Virginia state treasury employees found a T206 Wagner in an abandoned safe-deposit box. At first the state workers didn't know what they had.

"If it woulda been a snake, it woulda bit me," said Andy Henson of the treasurer's communications office. "I had no clue."

Henson got a clue fast, after the card was put on display at the state fair along with other unusual unclaimed property. A collector saw the display and informed state officials that the Gretzky card had just sold for $1.27 million. But unfortunately for West Virginia, an auction house quickly determined that the card was a reproduction that could have been printed anytime between 1920 and 1980. Writing on the original cards was red, while the West Virginia card was printed in black.

Then there are those who are just plain unlucky. Rosen remembers hearing from one inconsolable collector who found a pile of T206 cards, including a Wagner, in his attic. Unfortunately, a rat found the cards first. The cards were turned into what may be the rodent world's most expensive bedding.

Because T206 Wagners have always been far more valuable than other cards, they've been favorites of the hustlers, con men, and counterfeiters that have been hanging around the hobby for decades. In 1976 collectors Bob Rathgeber, Dick Reuss, and Tom Wickman made an announcement that roiled the hobby: They had found a previously unknown T206 Wagner issue, this time featuring a photo of the Flying Dutchman in an action pose. If true, it would have been revolutionary news. The only known T206 Wagners, of course, all featured Honus's familiar head-and-shoulders pose.

The collectors, who said they'd inadvertently picked up their rare find when they purchased a collection from a North Carolina man, planned on selling the card at the Detroit card convention that year. The twenty or so Wagner cards known to be in existence in 1976 were worth a then-whopping $2,500 to $3,000, according to a *Sporting News* column written by veteran *Daily News* baseball writer Bill Madden, and the trio of collectors hoped to sell their new find for at least that much. The collectors took the card to the Library of Congress, where an expert told them the card's paper dated back to 1910. Still, many collectors remained leery, and although this was before it became profitable to restore cards, skeptics said a card doctor had meticulously pasted the front from a less-valuable Wagner card printed by a candy company to a standard tobacco-card back.

"I guess the only way we could really find out if it is two different cards is to soak it in a sinkful of water for thirty minutes and then see if it peels apart," Rathgeber, then the director of publications for the Cincinnati Reds, told Madden. "I don't think I'd want to take that chance."

The hobby remained unconvinced, and Rathgeber and his partners finally submitted the card to the water test. The card peeled apart—or, as Madden so perfectly put it, "The great Wagner tobacco-card controversy has been officially put to rest. As the saying goes, it all came out in the wash." Rathgeber and his partners claimed they were victims and not perpetrators of attempted fraud. "I think it's safe to say that enough people know me in the hobby," Rathgeber told Madden. "They know I'm not trying to rip anyone off."

Rathgeber later pointed out that the hoax had an upside. It reinforced the head-and-shoulders T206 Wagner's status as the hobby's desirable card.

"It kinda leaves the original Wagner portrait as the prize in card collecting," Rathgeber told *Cincinnati Enquirer* sportswriter Bob Hertzel. "It would have destroyed the myth if ours had been legitimate."

Thirty years after Rathgeber's hopes for fame and fortune dissolved in a sinkful of water, two more Cincinnati men embarked on a twisted and frustrating journey to prove that they, too, belong in the exclusive club of T206 Wagner owners. For more than a decade, John Cobb and Ray Edwards have told anyone who would listen that they have a T206 Wagner that is almost as good as the Gretzky card. Cobb and Edwards believe that their card should sell for as much as $1 million. The only problem: Nobody in the hobby believes them. Bill Mastro and PSA president Joe Orlando have dismissed their card as an obvious reproduction, a cheap reprint, as fake as a three-dollar bill. Collectors and dealers, writing in hobby Internet forums, ripped Cobb and Edwards as a couple of cheap hustlers trying to peddle yet another counterfeit card on eBay.

Cobb and Edwards's critics shot back that there is an easy way for the two men to convince collectors the card is real: submit it to PSA or another grading service. Cobb and Edwards did talk to PSA about authenticating their card and grading its condition, but that discussion quickly turned into a nasty range war. PSA, like most grading companies, doesn't allow card owners to be present when their cards are evaluated, another grading practice that alarms some of the most elite of collectors. (One top collector said he would absolutely not let his cards out of his sight during the grading process.)

The grading companies say they are concerned about security—they don't want cards stolen—and they don't want owners trying to influence the grades their cards receive.

"We've graded twenty-three Wagner cards," Orlando said. "Our security measures are at the top of their game. We aren't going to sacrifice that for one customer."

Cobb and Edwards said that policy sounds reasonable for cards worth $15, $20, $100, even $1,000. But exceptions should be made for cards worth hundreds of thousands of dollars. How do they know PSA won't switch their card for another? How do they know PSA won't damage their card? "Would you let a one-million-dollar card out of your sight?" Edwards asked. "One scratch and the card loses a hundred thousand dollars in value."

A collector who owned a T206 Wagner put it a little more succinctly: "If I sent my card in to be slabbed, I'd make damned sure I was with them."

The controversy surrounding the Cobb-Edwards card became even more complicated by the issues of race and class. Cobb and Edwards are African-Americans from working-class backgrounds. They believe that the hobby—dominated by well-to-do white men—doesn't want a couple of black guys in the elite club that is T206 Wagner owners.

"There's a reason the big dogs in the industry want this card to go away," their attorney James Arnold said.

Some collectors said they brought up race and class to deflect attention from the possibility that their card is a fake, engaging in their own form of racism by bringing skin color into the controversy over their card in the first place. And Edwards seemed to go out of his way to pick fights with his critics. His posts on collectors' forums, pocked with misspellings and poor grammar, bristled with frustration and fury. He made an easy target. But some of the attacks posted on collector forums were filled with so much vitriol and rage that it is not hard to see why Cobb and Edwards feel embattled, why they felt like they never got a fair shake. What motivated such anger over a card so many collectors dismissed without a second thought? Why get so worked up over a card the collectors were positive no one would buy? In a hobby fraught with fraud and rip-offs, why spend so much time teeing off on a couple of marginal collectors like Cobb and Edwards?

"These are big-time playas in the vintage card arena," a collector named Jay Behrens taunted in response to an Edwards post on Network54, a popular vintage-card forum. "Didn't you read that he came up with the idea of fiber testing a card for authenticity? Come on, that's about as big a playa as you are gonna find."

A Network54 regular who identified himself as SGROSS posted this:

Race is the only reason these two jokers got their story told in the first place. Can you imagine if one of "us" (you know, old, fat, bald, white, smelly, tee-shirt wearing losers) walked into our local newspaper (be it the NY Times or EBF Gazette), and tried to get a story on our new Wagner find??? Hell, the receptionist and security guard would laugh us out the door before we got by the front desk. Sad: Two trusting soles [sic] who, once again, are beaten down by the man, with his evil knowledge and experience. Give me a break. They are an embarrassment to anyone who still believes in the legitimate struggles of the African-American in the USA. The absolute ignorance of their actions sets social Black images back to Stimey [sic] settin' on the stove wipen' [sic] his brow.

If Cobb and Edwards were truly a couple of con artists, as so many of the Network54 collectors and dealers said they were, they surely would have ditched their T206 Wagner years ago and moved on to something more profitable. They have spent years researching the T206 series, the American Tobacco Company, and turn-of-the-century printing techniques and paper. They carry dozens of thick binders and giant Tupperware tubs filled with data whenever they meet with someone to talk about their card. They have crisscrossed the Midwest visiting paper and printing experts. They have suffered humiliating setbacks, and they have endured the taunts and scorn of vintage-card collectors who take great delight in seeing them stumble. And yet they can't drop their quixotic effort to prove that their card is real.

"We've had a lot of sleepless nights with this card," Cobb said. "It's like we won the lottery and we can't cash the ticket."

Cobb and Edwards insist that their card has been thoroughly examined, undergoing far more scrutiny than any card in history, including the Gretzky T206 Wagner. But without the approval of PSA or another grading service, it is doubtful anybody will pay $100 for the card, never mind $1 million.

"Even if scientists say it's real, if it's not accepted by hobby experts, it will never sell in the hobby," said Steve Wolter, the owner of a Cincinnati memorabilia shop called Sports Investments.

The card itself is deeply stained, and its edges are dirty. Cobb and Edwards keep it encased between two three-by-six pieces of Lucite. Strips of aluminum foil protect both front and back—another rare Piedmont—from the damaging rays of the sun. Much like Bill Mastro with The Card, Cobb is vague about how he obtained his Wagner, and that has been held up as proof of fraud. Cobb said he got the card in 1983 or 1984—he's not exactly sure when—from an acquaintance who picked it up at an estate sale. Cobb doesn't remember the guy's name, but he does remember that the seller wanted $2,500, which was thousands of dollars less than the going price for a T206 Wagner in those days. The guy settled for $1,800, and Cobb can't explain why the seller was willing to let the card go at that bargain price. The seller promised that Cobb could get his money back if he couldn't turn it around. Soon after that, a collector offered Cobb $10,000 for Honus, but Cobb resisted the urge to sell.

"I thought if I held on to it for a while, maybe I could get $20,000 for it," he said. "I had to learn more. So I put the card away."

Collectors and dealers offer their own theories about the origins of the card. Brian Wentz, one of the brothers who run BMW Sports-cards, said he met Cobb and Edwards at a card show held at the Cincinnati Convention Center in 1992. They had bought a reprint of a T206 Wagner at the show and asked Wentz what he thought it was worth. When Wentz told them nothing—it's a reprint—he said they told him, "Just you wait. It's going to be worth something someday."

"That's bullshit. I've never been to a card show. That is just more bullshit from these Network54 guys," said Edwards, referring to the collector Internet forum.

A Newport, Kentucky, attorney named James Kidney called the Newport police after he learned that Cobb and Edwards were trying to sell the card on eBay in 2002. He told the cops he believed that the T206 Wagner they were selling was a reprint stolen from his law office eight months earlier. The police investigated but found no evidence of wrongdoing.

"That's more bullshit," an annoyed Edwards added. "He wouldn't have accused us of stealing his card if we were white."

Like Bill Mastro, John Cobb has the collecting gene. He was at one time a keyboard player in a band that included pioneering funk bassist Bootsy Collins—they once opened for Jimi Hendrix in a Cincinnati club—but mostly Cobb has spent his life collecting things. He worked as a trash collector when he was a teenager, and he would bring home things people had thrown out, fix them up, and resell them. As he got older, he started scouring garage sales, auctions, and flea markets for things he could clean up and sell for a profit, and at one point he had a half dozen storage bins filled with furniture, appliances, books, and toys.

In the early nineties, Cobb and Edwards were hanging out at Cobb's apartment watching magician David Copperfield tear up Wayne Gretzky's T206 Wagner on TV and then put it all back together again. "I've got that card," Cobb matter-of-factly told Edwards.

Edwards, the husband of Cobb's cousin, was stunned. The card that Copperfield had magically reconstructed was the most famous card in the world, purchased by Gretzky and his boss, then–Los Angeles Kings owner Bruce McNall, a year or so earlier for a whopping $451,000.

Edwards runs a Web site called RainbowsGold.com that sells health products and dietary supplements, and he is far more computer-savvy than Cobb. Eventually the two men formed a partnership: Cobb provided the card, and Edwards provided the computer know-how necessary to sell the T206 over the Internet.

"When I saw the card," said Edwards, "I got real excited. I said, 'We could do something with that card.' "

Cobb and Edwards attempted to sell their card on eBay several times. But they yanked the card twice because their minimum price—between $300,000 and $500,000—was not met. At least three other sales were halted, eBay spokesman Dean Jutilla said, because Cobb and Edwards's description of the card was vague. There were more questions about the authenticity of the T206 Wagner.

"What gets me is that eBay will let someone sell a piece of toast with Jesus's face on it," said James Arnold, their attorney. "But they won't let my guys sell this card."

Cobb and Edwards contacted PSA, but when they were told they couldn't be present when the card was examined, the situation turned ugly. PSA's Orlando suggested that the card was bogus in an interview with the *Cincinnati Enquirer*. Mastro said the card was a reprint because the *P* in "Pittsburg," which should have been slightly larger than the other letters, is the same size as the rest.

"Maybe it was a printer's error," Edwards said. "Maybe that's the way they did it at that particular factory. That's what makes this card unique."

Others complained that Wagner's image looked dull, as if it were a photocopy. Some said the discoloring on the card made it look like it had been dipped in coffee. There was no black border around the picture of Honus. One grading service did permit Cobb and Edwards to be present when the card was examined, and their findings were not good: Card Collector Services ruled that the Cobb-Edwards T206 Wagner was indeed a reprint. The Ohio men remained unbowed. In February 2003, Cobb and Edwards drove to Appleton, Wisconsin, home of Integrated Paper Services, an independent lab that provides testing and analysis of paper and other products.

For $303.50, IPS paper expert Walter Rantanen spent six hours analyzing the card. Rantanen reported that the Wagner's paper stock was consistent "with being from 1910." The T206 was free of titanium oxide, a whitening agent that wasn't introduced until 1921, Rantanen said.

"There were no red flags in the fibers," Rantanen added. "The paper stock was consistent with the time that card would have been made. There's nothing in there that shouldn't be there."

Cobb and Edwards then took the card to Arnie Schwed, an Ohio consultant to the paper industry. Schwed confirmed that the printing style was 1909 vintage in a letter to James Arnold. He expressed doubts that the card was sandwiched together like Rathgeber's T206, and he said the card was definitely not a counterfeit.

"In order for a counterfeiter to produce a card that would look like The Card, the skill of the printer would have to be of a master pressman with 5–10 years experience, and would require a machine which would cost between $500,000 and $2 million," Schwed wrote to Arnold. "However, even with a skilled pressman and necessary equipment, the paper of the card would not survive a printing press due to its age."

Finally Cobb and Edwards took their Honus to Binghamton, New York, where an appraiser and auctioneer named Bob Connelly valued the T206 Wagner at $850,000, based on the reports from Schwed and Rantanen. Armed with that new information, Cobb and Edwards again tried to sell their card on eBay in November 2005. But they had to shut down the sale almost as soon as it was listed. Edwards's eBay post quoted extensively from Connelly's report, a violation of their contract, which required them to reproduce all twenty pages in their entirety.

"If you only use sections of it," Connelly said, "it can be taken out of context."

But the card nagged at Connelly, a tall man with gray hair and the understated confidence of a country squire. He received ugly phone calls and e-mails from dealers and collectors who were furious that he had the gall to appraise Cobb and Edwards's card in the first place, much less put such a high value on it. He decided that maybe these guys weren't getting a fair shake. PSA and its sister companies, Connelly said, are certainly not infallible. He remembered submitting a Catfish Hunter signature from a consignor's autograph collection to PSA-DNA's QuickOpinion service. It came back as a forgery.

"This is a guy I trust, and he said, 'That can't be. I was there when he signed it.' That bothered me. What's happening is that we're getting into a situation where you can't sell a card unless you pay $100 to get it approved by one of four grading services. If you're not part of their clique, like John and Ray, you can't sell your card."

So when Edwards called Connelly a few months after their aborted eBay sale and asked if he would consider accepting the card for his auction, Connelly said yes. Another consignor had given him a cache of T206 cards to sell in his August 2006 auction. Cobb and Edwards's Wagner would be a perfect fit, and they could maximize their exposure by also offering the card on eBay. After so many years of frustration and rejection, things finally seemed to be working out for Cobb, Edwards, and their T206 Wagner. Not only was Connelly willing to take their card for his auction, but HBO's *Real Sports* program had decided to do a story on their crusade.

There was, however, a hitch. They had to deliver the T206 Wagner to Connelly so he could shop it around, show it off to prospective buyers. Cobb and Edwards would finally have to put the card in the hands of the graders in order to sell it. They were as edgy as mothers sending their toddler off to school for the very first time.

"We were definitely nervous," Edwards said. "But we had a good feeling about Bob. He was open-minded about the card. He had a good reputation, and when he gave us the appraisal, he put his neck on the line. Me and John discussed this for a long time, and we decided if we were ever going to sell this card, we had to trust somebody. We knew we couldn't trust PSA, because they had made up their minds without even seeing the card. We decided we could trust Bob."

Cobb and Edwards met Connelly at a rest stop in Cleveland, the halfway point between Cincinnati and Binghamton, to deliver the card, and Connelly went to work lining up potential bidders. The following week Connelly met a card dealer named Mike Mangasarian at the New York City offices of the Appraisers Association of America, twenty stories above Park Avenue South. Mangasarian, better known as Mike Mango, has long, dark hair and a big, bushy mustache that makes him look like a thin Gene Shalit, and he said that a prominent collector—whom he refused to identify—had hired him to check out the card and report back his opinion. With a crew from HBO filming the scene (the program would air on August 16), Connelly pulled the Cobb-Edwards card out of the pocket of his suit jacket and plopped it on a glass table.

"I figure it's a strong four," Connelly said, referring to the grade he thought it would receive from a card-grading service. "What's your opinion?"

"I agree," Mangasarian replied. "It's in that ballpark area."

And just like that, the most controversial baseball card in the hobby's recent history gained instant credibility. Mangasarian said he'd have to touch the card to verify its authenticity, but the $300,000 minimum bid didn't scare him away, and he said he'd be at the auction. Connelly said he lined up a couple of other interested collectors and dealers, too. Things appeared to be looking good for Cobb and Edwards. The hobby, however, remained quite skeptical. Some Network54 posters speculated that the paper and printing had tested correctly because the Cobb/Edwards Wagner was a skinned card—the back came from a real T206 while the front was a counterfeit. Others dismissed Schwed and Rantanen as shills and idiots. Many continued to bash Cobb and Edwards. Edwards fired back with an angry message to the board, demanding that his critics offer proof why they believed his T206 Wagner was a fraud.

Some collectors coolly laid out their reasoning. Others just got ugly. "You sound like someone that lives in the projects that wants to mooch off whitey while bad-mouthing whitey," a guy who identified himself as Freddy Sawyer wrote.

Many, however, called or e-mailed eBay and demanded that the giant online auction throw the card off their Web site, and eBay officials finally yanked it the day before the auction.

"If only Ray could have kept his fingers off the keyboards," Connelly said. "We could have sold that card."

Finally the day of the auction came. Connelly asked for someone to begin the bidding, and while the sounds of silence were gold for Simon and Garfunkel, they were lead for Cobb and Edwards: No one bid on the card at the auction. No one uttered a word. The silence was deafening. Cobb and Edwards looked wounded, their defeat and disappointment palpable to the HBO viewers who would watch their ordeal up close a few days later.

"I had a couple of collectors interested in the card, but they weren't interested after eBay pulled it," Connelly said. "When eBay pulled the card, they said it raised too many questions about its authenticity."

Mike Mangasarian did attend the auction, but when he finally got the chance to touch the card, he said it didn't feel right. It felt too glossy, too slick to be real. He admitted he hadn't done all his homework before meeting with Connelly in Manhattan a few weeks before the auction. "There were some things I should have been looking for," he said. "I wasn't as prepared as I should have been."

15

FAKES AND FRAUDS

The memorabilia industry is replete with tales of shady dealings, false advertising, and out-and-out fraud and thievery. Some of the tales are laughable, some are poignant, some shocking, some downright criminal. Some are all of the above.

Take the strange case of the Hall of Fame Heist.

On a summer day in 1972, a thief slipped into an exhibit room at the National Baseball Hall of Fame in Cooperstown, closed the door, removed six screws from the bottom of a wooden display case, and took out five baseballs—all autographed by presidents and now worth up to $1 million. The thief left a Cooperstown brochure in their place, put the top back on the display case, and escaped undetected.

"[He] was someone who came into the museum once or twice or three times and cased it," said Howard Talbot, director of the Hall of Fame between 1976 and 1993. "We had lost other things prior to that time. You didn't think of security in those days. You trusted people. You assumed they'd enjoy the exhibit and leave it for others to enjoy."

For years the Hall of Fame had been an easy mark for thieves, who stole everything from DiMaggio caps to historic documents. Some of these items, collectively now worth millions, were showing up in the booming sports-memorabilia and collectibles markets, and often in

Bill Mastro's auction catalogs. Then there was the Walter "Big Train" Johnson fiasco. Hank Thomas, Big Train's grandson, had made a pilgrimage to Cooperstown in October 1977 to learn more about his grandfather, who had won 416 games, second only to Cy Young's 511. As Billy Martin's Yankees battled the Dodgers in the World Series, Thomas went to the Hall of Fame to research the acclaimed biography he would publish in 1995, *Walter Johnson: Baseball's Big Train*.

"I was treated like some sort of royalty," he recalled.

But things turned uncomfortable when Thomas got to a room filled with presidential-related memorabilia. Thomas asked to see the Johnson exhibit, donated to Cooperstown by the Big Train's family in 1968. Five presidential baseballs, signed by Presidents Woodrow Wilson, William Howard Taft, Calvin Coolidge, Herbert Hoover, and Warren Harding for Big Train were gone from their wooden case in the center of the room. Cooperstown officials told Thomas two days later that the balls had been stolen five years before. The Taft ball alone could now fetch up to a half million dollars. Nobody had told Johnson's family.

"They had no answer why," Thomas said. "They were embarrassed. There was no investigation of any kind. None, zero. Their handling of the whole mess left a bad taste in my mouth."

The FBI, with the cooperation of Hall of Fame officials and professional baseball, investigated the heist. Four of the balls, which had been donated to the Hall by the Johnson family, were returned to the Hall in 2001, almost thirty years after they were stolen. Thomas had seen three of them in a Mastro Fine Sports Auction catalog.

"These baseballs are priceless," Hall president Dale Petroskey said when the balls were returned. Major League Baseball security recovered the remaining ball, signed by Harding, and returned it to Cooperstown in April 1999 after Hank Thomas spotted this one in a catalog offered by Ron Oser Enterprises, then a division of Mastro's company. Authorities didn't have enough evidence to file criminal charges in the case, and officials would not say who had the balls when they were recovered by the FBI.

Jeffery Wolfson, however, a Chicago securities-industry executive who collects sports and presidential memorabilia, surrendered the Taft ball to FBI investigators. Wolfson cooperated and was not a suspect in the case.

Wolfson said he did not know that the ball had been stolen. "I'm too naive," he said. "I'm one of these guys who assumes everybody is telling the truth."

He said he bought the ball for $25,000 from harness trainer Tom Harmer, whose clients had included Yankees owner George Steinbrenner. Harmer, who was not a suspect in the case, told the New York *Daily News* he bought two balls, the Taft and the Wilson, in 1997 for about $27,000 from Mr. Mint—New Jersey dealer Alan Rosen.

Rosen had bought the balls from Brooklyn collector Bill Hongach, a former Yankee batboy who told the *Daily News* that he bought three of them in 1975 for about $800 at a Manhattan card show from a man carrying a brown grocery bag filled with memorabilia.

Wolfson wasn't reimbursed for the Taft ball, but at least he was able to use its value—appraised at $125,000—as a tax deduction.

The whole affair was an embarrassment to Cooperstown, which has enhanced its security measures to keep the Ruth jerseys and DiMaggio bats from walking out the door. Shortly before the Johnson baseballs were stolen, someone removed a Joe DiMaggio cap from a display locker. Hall officials replaced it with another cap, this time attached to the locker with a wire. Someone used a wire cutter to snag that one. Officials put Plexiglas over the front display of lockers, but souvenir hunters would pull corners of jerseys through air vents and snip off a swatch of baseball history. Items stamped with Hall of Fame–numbered logos were common at memorabilia shows, including one that Josh Evans of Lelands bought in 1988 from Mike Gutierrez, an authenticator for Mastro and the card expert who had raised questions about the Gretzky T206 Wagner after it was graded by PSA: The Babe Ruth photo had a Hall of Fame stamp on the back covered with typewriter Wite-Out. Evans notified the Hall and the FBI, which later questioned him about where he got the photo. Prosecutors declined to pursue the matter. The Hall of Fame would find itself in another uncomfortable situation in 2001 when word got around that the glove used to make what might have been the most spectacular catch in World Series history, a play that not only robbed the great Joe DiMaggio of a game-tying home run but provoked the Yankee Clipper into uncharacteristically kicking the dirt as he headed for second, was on the memorabilia market and expected to go for as much as $100,000, according to the authenticator who was appraising it—MastroNet's Mike Guiterrez. Al Gionfriddo, the man who made the jaw-dropping catch in Yankee Stadium in Game 6 of the 1947 World Series, was telling people that he'd been told by Guiterrez that he could get six figures for the glove he used to make the catch. So Gionfriddo, who was then seventy-nine years old and looking to provide for his family, put the mitt into an auction run by MastroNet. Gionfriddo said he hoped to give the proceeds to his four grown children.

"It's easier to divide money than to cut a glove up four ways," said Gionfriddo, who died in 2003. "My wife thought the guy was blowing smoke, but I thought it might get at least $40,000."

There was just one catch: According to the Hall of Fame, Gionfriddo had already donated the glove to Cooperstown in 1974, where it is displayed in the World Series room next to the one Willie

Mays used for his famous over-the-shoulder catch of Vic Wertz's blast in 1954. Certainly the glove represented one of the most famous catches in baseball history. In Game 6, with the Dodgers leading 8–5, but down three games to two in the Series, Brooklyn manager Burt Shotton put Gionfriddo into left field for defensive purposes in the sixth inning. Dodgers pitcher Joe Hatten walked a batter and then, with two outs, gave up a single to Yogi Berra. The next man up, DiMaggio, sent Hatten's first pitch screaming toward the left-field fence. Gionfriddo grabbed the ball at the 415-foot mark as it was about to drop over into the bullpen.

Red Barber described the play on the radio this way: "There's a deep drive to left field, back goes Gionfriddo, back, back, back, back, he makes a one-handed catch against the bullpen. Oh, doctor!" DiMaggio, by then approaching second, kicked at the base path, the only time anyone ever saw him display frustration on the field."

No question, the glove we have is the one Gionfriddo used to make the catch," said Jeff Idelson, a spokesman for the Hall of Fame, which stood by its claim that the glove in the Hall, not the one in a MastroNet auction catalog, was the one used to make the catch.

So how did Al Gionfriddo, by all accounts a nice, honest man whose only real claim to fame was that catch, come to auction off a glove he'd already donated to the Hall of Fame? Many believe that Guiterrez convinced the aging and ailing Gionfriddo to put the glove—or *a* glove—on the market. A MastroNet spokeswoman said in 2001 that Gionfriddo supplied an affidavit claiming that the glove in the auction was the one he used in the '47 Series and that he had provided the company with a copy of a letter he sent to the Hall of Fame saying the glove on display was not the real deal. But the Hall believed otherwise, based on a 1947 letter from its former director, the late Ken Smith, thanking Gionfriddo's old friend Leonard

Robelotto for delivering the glove. The letter reads, "It is a genuine historic object—Al Gionfriddo's glove—appreciated in this institution." Smith could have mistakenly believed that the glove was from "The Catch," but because Gionfriddo's career was hardly stellar, it is doubtful the astute Smith would have accepted a glove unless it was the famous one. The Hall's Idelson said his organization also authenticated the glove by comparing it with film clips of the play.

Bidders apparently suspected that something was awry. The glove that Gutierrez, MastroNet's authenticator, said would sell for $100,000 or more went for only $12,329.15. The buyer was Gionfriddo's wife, Sue.

"We didn't want to let it go to someone else for that little money," Gionfriddo said. "We wanted to keep it in the family."

Gionfriddo said he was so fed up with memorabilia auctions that he would give Cooperstown the glove he'd tried to sell and let them sort out which is the one he used to rob "Joltin' Joe." He was undoubtedly embarrassed by the whole incident, which in many ways tarnished his big-league moment.

"It won the game for us," Gionfriddo said of his catch. "People compare it to Willie Mays's in 1954, but he had a lot more room to make his catch. I was up against the fence. And he caught a ball hit by Vic Wertz. Mine was hit by Joe DiMaggio."

Their pockets bulging with cash, memorabilia collectors flocked to New York from every corner of Baseball Nation in 1999 to battle over the legendary wares put up for sale by Yankee minority owner Barry Halper, who had assembled the most extensive collection in history after fifty years of wheeling and dealing and cajoling everyone from the players to the clubbies to the managers and owners to give up their goods. The weeklong auction at Sotheby's racked up

$25 million, selling everything from a Rickey Henderson jersey to a jar of Vaseline autographed by Gaylord Perry to a glove Mickey Mantle supposedly used—circa 1960—and it propelled Rob Lifson to stardom.

North Carolina collector Ralph Perullo arrived at Sotheby's with his eye on Lot Number 1118, advertised as the Rawlings Red Rolfe glove used by the great Joe DiMaggio during the late 1930s. Joltin' Joe even vouched for the glove himself: It was accompanied by an index card that said, "This glove was used in my first years as a Yankee—Joe DiMaggio." But then Perullo ran into glove expert Dennis Esken at the auction, and his excitement turned to disgust. Esken told Perullo the glove wasn't even manufactured until 1954—three years after DiMaggio retired: The glove had lacing through the fingers, a sure sign it was a postwar model. Perullo backed off bidding on the mitt.

"If Joe were standing next to me, I'd shake his hand and tell him he was a hell of a ballplayer," said Esken, who is regarded as the nation's top authority on baseball mitts. "I'd also tell him he's no glove expert."

But the disease that had infected the hobby was spreading: The misidentified glove remained on the trading circuit long after the Halper sale, backed up by a letter of authenticity from the hobby's most influential evaluators, Dave Bushing and Dan Knoll, whose seal of approval can make or break an item's sale price. All told, after it had been bought that September day by the Upper Deck trading card company for $34,500 and used for a promotional contest, the glove was sold at least twice more and brought in thousands of dollars to its auctioneers and consignors before finally being pulled off the market in 2003. It was returned to Sotheby's, the auction house that originally sold it.

The authenticators tried to distance themselves from the glove. Even though his name was on the certificate authenticating the glove, Knoll later said he had never examined it, and Bushing denied authenticating any of the seven gloves offered in the Halper auction, a claim Lifson would dispute. Hired by Sotheby's to work the sale, Lifson said that Bushing authenticated all the gloves in the Halper auction, and Upper Deck also said it relied on Bushing's expertise before buying the glove. Upper Deck spokesman Don Williams said that Bushing assured the company the glove was genuine. "We acted on the advice of Bushing and Sotheby's," he said. Lifson would later claim that he, too, relied on Sotheby's and Bushing to authenticate Halper's massive trove.

In spite of the controversy surrounding the glove, it continued to move through the channels of the hobby. The winner of the Upper Deck contest placed the glove in Lifson's 2001 Robert Edward Auction sale. It turned up again in a 2002 auction conducted by MastroNet, whose president, Doug Allen, said he asked the buyer to return the glove in 2003, after a knowledgeable collector notified the company about a potential problem. Having determined that the glove wasn't manufactured until the 1950s, MastroNet said it reimbursed its customer. "If the guy got his money back, what does it matter now?" Allen asked.

Esken begged to differ. "This is *not* a hobby, it's a business, dictated by a few individuals who determine what is real and what it is worth," Esken said. "If it was real, it would have sold for hundreds of thousands of dollars. A lot of people knew that—but apparently not everybody."

The role Bushing and Knoll played in the glove's many sales is what troubles self-appointed memorabilia watchdog Robert Plancich. Their letter of authenticity accompanying the glove at the 2001

Robert Edward Auction and the 2002 MastroNet sale gave it the Good Housekeeping Seal of Approval in the mind of the general public.

"If these guys are this sloppy with a DiMaggio glove—something that is a real piece of American history—then how much time do they spend on less-significant items?" asked Plancich. "This brings into question every item they have supposedly painstakingly authenticated."

Plancich is a high-school umpire from Arcadia, California, and the memorabilia industry's loudest critic, a whistle-blower who has mounted a tireless crusade to clean up the hobby. He is viewed by some as a hero bent on reforming an industry plagued by hustles and conflicts of interest. Others call him an abrasive blowhard who irresponsibly attacks the industry's most respected auction houses, authenticators, and dealers. Memorabilia's elite suffered Plancich's attacks in silence for years, privately dismissing him as an angry crackpot with no credibility.

But in late 2004 somebody finally hit back: Louisville Slugger manufacturer Hillerich & Bradsby sued Plancich in Los Angeles Superior Court, seeking an end to his confrontational campaign questioning the authenticity of a bat purportedly used by DiMaggio during his legendary 56-game hitting streak. H&B, which had bought the bat for $345,000 at a MastroNet auction, claimed that Plancich's relentless criticism delayed its plans to display the bat at its Louisville Slugger Museum. "Each day that the museum delays display of the bat, H&B loses money through loss of museum guests," the suit said, although it failed to explain exactly how Plancich was preventing the company from exhibiting the bat. Bushing, who had authenticated and consigned the bat, chimed in with applause for the lawsuit. "He's been throwing mud at people for so long, it's time for him to back it up," Bushing said.

But some collectors and dealers were quietly applauding Plancich for another reason: They believed that Hillerich & Bradsby was trying to silence Plancich, a former accountant who had left a job at Arthur Andersen to care for his elderly mother and was getting by on savings and the money he earns refereeing youth sports. They knew he didn't have the resources to hire a lawyer to fight H&B, and that even if he did prevail, other battles would loom: MastroNet had been considering legal action against him, too. Esken called the lawsuit an attempt to silence an industry critic, someone who was costing the hobby's big players business. The issue, once again, had come down to the amorphous nature of collectibles—there was no hard evidence, no real evidence of any kind, proving that DiMaggio had used the bat during the streak. Prominent Denver collector Marshall Fogel summed it up perfectly: "There's no question it's debatable. It just depends on what side you want to fall on it. Louisville Slugger made the choice to believe the bat is real."

Once again Dave Bushing was at the center of a controversy. Unknown to H&B, not only had Bushing authenticated the DiMaggio bat, but he was also its seller. It was widely known that Bushing had extensively researched the bat and given it his highest mark, an A-10, meaning that its provenance was indisputable, but he failed to divulge that he was also selling it, creating what must surely be one of the most egregious conflicts of interest to hit the hobby in years, a conflict H&B discovered only when contacted by a reporter.

Plancich had begun his crusade several years earlier, after several autographed baseballs he'd hoped to consign to an auction were rejected as forgeries. Disgusted, he formed the Collectors Alliance for Reform and Disciplinary Sanctions (CARDS), a one-man group dedicated to cleaning up the industry. He threw himself into his campaign with a fury, contacting the press and law-enforcement agencies demanding investigations and contacting dealers, authenticators, and auction houses he believed were offering questionable memorabilia to the public. In one of his e-mails to H&B, he wrote that the company would be crossing a line that "I am sure you don't want to cross" if it displayed the DiMaggio bat and, in effect, defrauded the public.

Plancich got some measure of vindication when, in March 2005, a California judge dismissed the suit, ruling that Plancich's criticism of the bat was protected by the First Amendment and that H&B had not demonstrated probability that it could win the case. Plancich's attorney had also argued that California's anti-SLAPP statute (SLAPP stands for "strategic lawsuit against public participation"), which protects whistle-blowers, covered Plancich, too.

"I don't buy it when a leap of faith puts $345,000 into an authenticator's pocket," Plancich said after the suit was dismissed.

But the battle was not without cost to Planich. He paid attorneys' fees, lost sleep, said he was intimidated by the industry giants. There was one bit of consolation, though: As a result of Plancich's unrelenting criticism, Bushing's authentication service now informs clients when it owns a piece it is authenticating.

The DiMaggio glove finally made its way back to Sotheby's, and even though virtually everyone involved in the mitt's travels now agrees that it's a 1950s glove and was not used by DiMaggio in a major-league game, the Upper East Side auction house wouldn't say if it sought compensation from Halper, who was ill at the time. But Sotheby's did ask Bob Clevenhagen, the senior glove designer for Rawlings, for his opinion.

"To anybody who knows anything about gloves, it's black and white," Clevenhagen said. "This glove was made in the fifties."

The DiMaggio glove raised what was becoming a hot issue—the

credibility of authenticators. In 2005, SCD Authentic, the firm Bushing worked for, revised another of its practices and determined that it would issue signatures only from authenticators who actually reviewed the items. But Plancich believed that the practice that resulted in a fraudulent DiMaggio glove's returning to the market time and time again was so widespread that almost no changes in policy could save the hobby. He recounted a conversation he had with Bushing about the DiMaggio glove a few years ago in which the authenticator told him that the glove itself was insignificant.

"The value is the letter," Plancich remembers Bushing telling him. "You can always get another glove.'"

The DiMaggio glove is not the most infamous purchase in the Halper auction. That honor belongs to the movie actor and comedian Billy Cyrstal, who in 1999 shelled out $239,000 for a questionable Mickey Mantle glove in a embarrassing transaction that continues to dog Crystal and the hobby.

Esken described the scene at the Halper auction as electric, with the buzz peaking over a game-used Mickey Mantle glove, advertised as "circa 1960" and valued in the Sotheby's catalog at $10,000 to $20,000. After some furious bidding, the glove went to Crystal, the director of the Mantle-Maris home-run-chase movie *61**, for a whopping $239,000.

"Can I jump from here?" Esken remembered a shell-shocked Crystal asking as he brandished the bidding paddle from his skybox. "Please, don't let my mother know how much I paid for this glove."

But four years later, on the eve of an auction of three hundred pieces put up for sale by Mantle's family, memorabilia insiders were saying that Crystal's buyer's remorse may have been prophetic. His

$239,000 glove hadn't come from the height of Mantle's career, as Sotheby's "circa 1960" description indicated; most likely the glove was used in 1966, when the injury-plagued slugger appeared in just 108 games and the Yankees finished in last place in the American League.

It was a typical error in what was quickly becoming a scandal-stained industry. Authentication problems were rampant, the conflicts of interest among dealers, authenticators, and auction houses staggering. "Buyer beware" was the watchword of the day, and collectors were calling for reform. Crystal, meanwhile, was phoning Rawlings's Clevenhagen to ask what year his glove was manufactured. Clevehagen confirmed what Crystal already knew by telling him, "Made no earlier than 1964 and most likely used in 1966."

Crystal also picked Clevenhagen's brain about a Mantle mitt that was auctioned in 2003 by Guernsey's in the Convention Center at Madison Square Garden. The Guernsey's collection represented a hodgepodge of the significant and the mundane in Mantle's life—his bankbook, credit cards, and pay stubs. Two of his three MVP awards and his 1962 World Series ring and the Babe Ruth Sultan of Swat Award that Mantle won in 1956, his Triple Crown year. The material was coming from Mantle's family, so it was assumed by the public that the goods were authentic. But, as was the case with DiMaggio, even the player and his family can be mistaken.

In a related incident, a glove Halper had acquired from Cy Young's estate was purchased at the Sotheby's auction by collector Kevin Keating for $71,000, but Keating's money was refunded two months later, when he returned the glove after learning that it was not used by the great pitcher but probably belonged to his grandson. Sotheby's admitted to making an error.

In the Crystal situation, however, the auction house was never willing to concede that it had erred when it described the Crystal glove as "circa 1960." Its authenticators, they said, could not determine the specific year Mantle used the glove, and they cited Halper's own testimonial that Mantle himself had told Halper he'd used it "in 1958. I never intended to misidentify it."

Esken and other collectors were a bit more skeptical. They'd known for years that Crystal hadn't gotten what he thought he was buying, although that particular discrepancy didn't become public until Guernsey's president Arlan Ettinger began preparing for his own auction of the Mantle-family glove in December 2003. Ettinger called Rawlings for information about that glove, and Clevenhagen told him it was probably used during the 1963 season. Ettinger told the glove designer that in that case Crystal's glove, with its elaborate signature, was probably made toward the end of Mantle's career. The Mantle-family mitt has Mickey's simple autograph from the first part of his career embossed on it, while the Crystal glove has the more elaborate signature from his last years with the Yankees. Clevenhagen said the new signature hadn't shown up in his catalog until 1965.

The hobby is still debating Crystal's purchase. The word "circa" gives a year or two of leeway, some believe. Others say that the cachet of a sale like Halper's or the Mantle auction can dramatically increase the value of an item. "This isn't like real estate—you can't compare the price of a glove to a similar glove," Esken said. "Every auction is different. This glove is worth whatever Billy Crystal thinks it is worth."

One thing was certain, though: The value of memorabilia was being determined by factors other than authenticity.

A WHITE KNIGHT

Rob Lifson lives in a leafy New Jersey suburb, thirty miles west of Manhattan, where kids ride their bikes down the sidewalks and SUVs and Volvo station wagons line the driveways. In the basement of his pristine new house, Lifson rules his empire, Robert Edward Auctions, among the most prestigious sports-memorabilia auction houses in America. He is a boyish-looking forty-six, reserved, bookish, with a slight stammer. His employees spend their days examining collections, taking photos, setting prices, writing and editing copy, and assembling the gorgeous color catalogs that feature the items in his yearly auctions. Lifson himself wages a daily battle for respectability, fighting against the evils that lurk within the hobby— the shill bidders, the card doctors, the conflicted, all combined into what he calls "the pink elephant in the room."

Lifson split with Mastro in late 2002, seventeen years after that drive to Sevchuk's hobby shop in Hicksville, finally severing the relationship that had lasted from junior high through the merger of Robert Edward Auctions and MastroNet in 2000. He got a modest sum for his 30 percent interest in the company but felt like he'd won the lottery, or at least walked out of a fog with a clear path ahead. Lifson remains close to Gidwitz and they have joined together in a below-the-radar fight to clean up the hobby. Gidwitz wrote a letter for Lifson's September 2004 auction, a missive directed at Mastro and intended to help direct business toward the man he considers the most trustworthy and honest in the business. It caused a stir in the hobby and Gidwitz is as proud of that letter as he is of any one of his uncut Goudey sheets. "If I've been wronged, he takes it personally," Gidwitz said of Lifson.

> Dear Robert Edward Auctions:
>
> The purpose of this letter is to write a letter of recommendation for your services to others. As a collector who occasionally has gotten more than my share of attention, people are always asking me if I can recommend any auction service for selling their materials. I am not an easy customer. I have very high standards about how business should be conducted. I take making any formal recommendation very seriously. That is why it is so important for me to communicate my respect for the unrivaled quality of Robert Edward Auctions' extraordinary service. I appreciate the incredible job Robert Edward Auctions has always done for me in selling materials from my personal collection. Whether you were helping me sell the famous T206 Wagner for over a million dollars or an oddball lot that sells for only $500, I have always been overwhelmed in every way with the quality of your service and the results. . . . I consider Robert Edward Auctions to be the finest auction service in the hobby. In an industry with an endless amount of problems, conflicts of interest, and even out and out fraud, Robert Edward Auctions is a beacon of light. . . . I know I am not alone in saying that the policies of most of your competitors, which are rarely held up to scrutiny by buyers, sellers or

the media have made me uncomfortable even participating in most auctions these days. . . . Simply put, I would never trust my most valuable material to any other auction house. I have even put Robert Edward Auctions in my will. It is an honor for me to recommend Robert Edward Auctions to all without reservation and a pleasure to know that in doing so I am helping to steer collectors in the right direction.

    Michael Gidwitz

One of those personal slights occurred when Gidwitz tried to sell a Chicago Cubs display piece he purchased through Mastro Auctions, called *Yard of the Cubs*, a scene depicting the playing field, some players, and a Cubbie bear. Gidwitz gave Lifson the piece to auction, and as he was examining it, Lifson began to get the feeling that something was wrong with the set. "So I found a book with the scene, and I see it!" he said. "I felt stupid—there's a side trimmed off. If all you ever had was the one, you might not think about it, that it's missing a part of it. It didn't fall off—somebody cut it off. Someone had intentionally doctored it. Can I tell you I know Bill did that? No. Should Bill have known? I would think he should know. There's no gray area. Maybe he would say, 'When I sold it to him, I told him.'" Lifson had to deliver the bad news to Gidwitz. "I had to say, 'Mike, I don't really want it in the auction.'"

In Lifson's view, one of the biggest problems facing the hobby is the pervasiveness of one particularly unsavory practice: shill bidding. In his catalogs and on his Web site, RobertEdwardAuctions.com, Lifson goes to great lengths to assure his customers that neither he nor his employees will bid anonymously on items to drive up the price, a tactic that would seem so blatantly dishonest as to be criminal, and certainly something you shouldn't have to address in your marketing campaign. Nonetheless, many houses are known to use shill bidders, and Lifson felt it important to separate himself from what he believes is a common practice.

Under the heading "No Conflicts of Interest" on his Web site, Lifson has delineated the ills of the industry, from auction houses that bid on material in their own auctions, to shill bidding, to selling their own wares at their auctions.

We are not dealers. Robert Edward Auctions will never place a bid on material in our own auction. Robert Edward Auctions will never purchase material outright to offer at auction. With Robert Edward Auctions, bidders are guaranteed that they never have to worry about the auction house bidding against them on any lot in the auction—EVER. With Robert Edward Auctions, bidders also never have to worry about secret hidden reserves—EVER.

You will never see a "Wanted to Buy" ad placed by Robert Edward Auctions. . . . These firm policies translate directly into greater and well deserved bidder confidence, and in turn higher prices for consignors. Many auctions are run by dealers offering material they own. This common practice exposes consignors and bidders to numerous conflicts—conflicts which can and do cost bidders and consignors money, and can ultimately make bidders uncomfortable even participating in the auction.

These are conflicts that DO NOT EXIST with Robert Edward Auctions.

Under no circumstances does Robert Edward Auctions, LLC allow for a "house account" to bid on lots in the auction. Under no circumstances are executives or employees of Robert Edward Auctions, LLC permitted to place bids in the auc-

tion. Under no circumstances are consignors permitted to bid
on their own lots. This is a consignment auction, conducted
by Robert Edward Auctions, LLC on behalf of consignors.

Under no circumstance is material offered at auction by
Robert Edward Auctions, LLC owned in part or whole by
Robert Edward Auctions, LLC. . . . Everyone likes an honest
auction.

Lifson has worked with the FBI on investigations into the authenticity of baseball cards and memorabilia as well as practices within
the industry, and he has testified in court on behalf of the Department of Justice. He refused to discuss the government's latest foray
into sports collectibles—an investigation into "Coingate," the scandal
involving Ohio coin dealer Tom Noe—which has also entangled Bill
Mastro in its wide net. Noe was the Bush-Cheney campaign chairman
in northwest Ohio in the 2004 election, and he raised more than
$100,000 for the president's reelection bid. He also convinced Ohio
Bureau of Workers Compensation officials to give him $50 million to
invest in two rare-coin funds. But instead of investing the money, Noe
used it to further his political network and bankroll his lavish lifestyle. On October 27, 2005, Noe was indicted in a federal investigation on counts of conspiracy, campaign contribution violations, and
false statements. On May 31, 2006, Noe reversed an earlier plea and
pleaded not guilty. In November 2006 he was found guilty of stealing
more than $1.1 million from the coin funds he managed for the state,
and on September 12, Noe was sentenced to a term of twenty-seven
months for each of the three felony charges, including illegally fun-
neling money to President Bush's campaign, to be served concur-
rently. He was also fined $136,200 and ordered to serve two years of
supervised release and two hundred hours of community service

upon his release. He was allowed to remain free on bail pending disposition of state felony charges against him.

When authorities searched Noe's Vintage Coins and Collectibles in Maumee, Ohio, they found a cache of sports memorabilia, including Bob Gibson–signed baseballs, and records showing that Mastro Auctions had sold at least $1.3 million worth of memorabilia to Noe's fund. The lots included Hall of Fame plaques purchased for $16,541, a Mickey Mantle bat ($14,014), a collection of ten thousand baseball cards ($8,603), one hundred balls signed by Ted Williams ($29,078), and twelve Walter Payton–signed footballs ($4,016).

Investigators believed that Noe had purchased much of the material with state money and that he'd bought much of it from Mastro Auctions. They grew suspicious as they examined scores of transactions between Noe and Mastro's company, according to Lucas County prosecutor John Weglian and William Brandt, president of Development Specialists, the company hired by Ohio to liquidate the coin investment. (The FBI, however, has initiated an investigation into shill bidding within the collectibles industry: Around Thanksgiving 2006, an unmarked car arrived at the home of a well-known collector, and the driver, an FBI agent, came with a list of questions centering on the practice.)

Investigators are trying to determine why Noe paid exorbitant prices for some of the items he purchased with the money from the workers' comp fund. One possible explanation, according to authorities, is that Noe was the victim of shill bidding. But authorities haven't ruled out the possibility that Mastro may have split the profits with the shamed Republican Party leader. One person subpoenaed by Ohio authorities said Noe had a secret account with Mastro Auctions and that only Bill Mastro was allowed to conduct transactions with

Noe. Of course, none of that would surprise Lifson. He has seen too much, heard too much, of what is perpetrated by people in the hobby. He decided he would not follow the industry path, no matter where it would have taken him.

Lifson's cold war with Mastro has its roots in what has happened in the hobby since that day in 1985 when they drove Lifson's old green Honda back toward Philadelphia, with the future of the hobby—and their own futures—in Mastro's briefcase. Lifson himself is no choirboy—he is a successful businessman, an expert in a cutthroat field, nobody's fool.

But that was long ago, and years later Lifson has seen the devastation, walked among the wreckage. Since his split with Mastro, he has built his business on the good faith he offers his customers. He recently added to the message on his Web site by sending an e-mail to those on his mailing list. In the e-mail he noted that in recent weeks he'd received a number of consignments in which the graded cards had clearly been doctored. The card doctors, he wrote, have become "so brazen" as to alter cards that had already been sold by Robert Edward Auctions, in some cases only months before. The cards had been "significantly altered, reholdered, and now grade higher, according to the grading label." All the consignors were unaware that the cards had been altered, he wrote, but nonetheless his auction house would have to disclose its information before selling a card. Some consignors asked to have their cards returned, including one $10,000 card. Lifson went further in his message: "And while it is bad enough that the altering of cards is an epidemic, it is particularly disturbing that some of the most sophisticated 'work' on cards (including the previously mentioned $10,000 card) has actually been executed by employees of auction houses that also deal in cards."

Lifson declined to name names in his e-mail but his missive set off an explosion on the hobby's Network54 collector forum, with speculation running rampant about which houses were doing the doctoring. For his part, Lifson denied fingering anyone, including Mastro, but in a Network54 post in late November, Doug Allen responded to questions put directly to him about altering cards. Allen admitted that Mastro Auctions does some altering—laying down corners that may have been flipped during handling; removing paste, glue, and light marks—but denied that extensive work is done to the cards that come through the house. As for trimming cards, Allen said flatly that he is "totally against trimming cards." The debate went on for several days and elicited scores of heated responses from some of the hobby's most serious collectors.

Lifson is convinced that his cleanup campaign is the only way the collectibles industry can right itself and survive. There is too much graft, too much fraud, too much money being changed in too few hands to think otherwise. Lifson put what is going on in simple terms. "It's called stealing," he said.

You don't have to look far—Coingate, Robert Plancich's battle in California, the accusations of racism and insider dealing from Ray Edwards and John Cobb in Cincinnati—to realize that the days of the Wild West are no longer unchecked. It's getting more difficult for yesterday's outlaw to become today's sheriff, especially when the lawsuits are piling up and the cops are looking over your shoulder. Which is exactly what happened to Tony Cocchi. Cocchi, a broker who supplied high-end memorabilia to Mastro Auctions, Lelands, and other houses and dealers, was indicted on a theft-by-deception charge by a Cobb County, Georgia, grand jury in September 2006. Prosecutors referred the case to the grand jury after Goodman Espy, a prominent Atlanta obstetrician with an extensive sports-memorabilia collection, told them that Cocchi had sold him a bogus Ty Cobb jersey.

Cocchi is a "bird dog," someone who prowls the flea markets for collections and scours the obituary pages for players' deaths, hoping to hit the lottery, maybe find a Cobb jersey, or, if hell freezes over, a Wagner T206. But Cocchi had built up a strong network of retired players and their families who would contact him when they were ready to sell their collections, and he was not viewed as a thief. Espy had purchased the jersey from Cocchi in 1991 for $85,000 and had decided in 2005 to finally sell it and donate the proceeds to the Salvation Army's Hurricane Katrina fund. He figured that it might bring as much as $200,000, but he needed a certificate from an established authentication service before he could consign the jersey to Mastro Auctions. That's when his troubles began. Memorabilia Evaluation and Research Services rejected the jersey as a fake, claiming that its manufacturer never supplied big-league jerseys. Espy demanded his money back from Cocchi, who refused to return it. The investigation has sent a shudder around the hobby.

"There's never been a fear of penalties in this business," said Darrel O'Mary, the dealer who introduced Cocchi to Espy fifteen years ago. "There's always been a wink and a nod about these things. It may take throwing some people in jail to clean this up."

Espy was simply fed up with the fraud. "Too much of this hobby is driven by greed," he said. "We need someone to come in and police this, because the industry can't police itself. I got screwed. A lot of people are getting screwed, and I'm tired of it."

That Cocchi wasn't known as one of the bad guys, the true grifters who are in the business to shake down the public through anonymous sales on eBay or other auction houses, seemed to rattle the hobby more than other recent scandals. Cocchi had been around for more than twenty years, starting out as a card collector in the 1970s. But there was another side to the Cocchi story, one that had widely circulated in the hobby for years. As part of his investigation into the Espy jersey, Marietta police detective Ricky Redd began looking into a transaction Cocchi had made several years earlier, when he paid an exorbitant amount at a Lelands auction for a collection of batting-practice balls from Philadelphia's old Connie Mack Stadium. Lelands president Mike Heffner said Cocchi's unusual interest in the lot raised questions in his mind, so he marked some of the balls with discreet dots before shipping them to Cocchi. The dotted balls, he said, later wound up in auctions and at memorabilia shows advertised as Hank Aaron homers and other historically significant balls.

"We have tried to get these balls off the market," Heffner said. "Unfortunately, some of them were already sold."

Espy intended to pursue the case as far as it would go. "I'm willing to do whatever it takes to help the hobby get its ship straightened out," he said. "Issues like this need to be publicized. If there's a risk you'll be arrested or indicted for selling bad memorabilia, maybe guys won't do it."

MILLION-DOLLAR BABY

At an age when most young men are still trying to figure out what to do with their lives, Brian Seigel was making mountains of money. Shortly after he graduated from Cal State Fullerton in 1983, Seigel invested $1,000 in Rockford Industries, a company he founded with several partners that offers financing for health-care providers to buy medical equipment and computers. Seigel put in seventy-hour workweeks for several years, and his investment paid off—by 1990, *Inc.* magazine was touting Rockford as one of the nation's five hundred fastest-growing companies.

Seigel was born in Toronto in 1960 and moved to Orange County, California, with his family when he was two years old. Like a lot of boys, he collected baseball cards, but baseball wasn't even his favorite sport—he preferred hockey and basketball—and when he grew up, he pretty much forgot about the hobby. But in the mid-1980s, Seigel jumped back in again, collecting the cards of baseball players he had idolized as a little boy playing ball on a Southern California cul-de-sac with his brother Mitch and their friends in the 1960s. Those cards sparked his interest in more vintage cards, and he started working backward, first adding 1950s cards to his collection. By the early nineties, the amateur historian was collecting prewar cards. By the late nineties, Seigel had worked his way back to the turn of the twentieth century and had put together one of the finest T206 collections in the world.

"I like the history of baseball and I've learned a lot about it through collecting," Seigel said in a 2001 interview.

Seigel fantasized about buying the Gretzky T206 when Florida postal worker Patricia Gibbs auctioned it off in 1996 and, even earlier, when Jim Copeland had sold it in 1991. He didn't have hundreds of thousands of dollars to spend on a baseball card, however, so he sat those auctions out. But Rockford Industries went public in 1995, and in 1999 the company was sold to American Express for $61 million. At the age of forty, Seigel suddenly had the money and the time to buy whatever cards he wanted.

And what he wanted was a T206 Wagner, and not just any Wagner. He wanted the Gretzky T206 Wagner. He wanted The Card.

"When Rockford Industries was sold to American Express in 1999, that gave me the resources to become serious about the hobby," Seigel said. "It's all discretionary income."

So when Michael Gidwitz decided to sell his T206 Wagner through Robert Edward Auctions and eBay in 2000, Seigel vowed that he'd be a contender. He set a price limit for himself and vowed not to go past that figure, but at least this time he'd be in the game.

The bidding started at $500,000 on July 5, 2000; by July 14 there were seven bids, with the top bidder offering $800,000. Five more bids came the next and final day. Seigel, eager to become the first person to spend a million bucks on a baseball card, bid $900,000 on July 15. The buyer's fee would have pushed the total price past the $1 million mark. Seigel relaxed, confident that nobody would top him.

But in the waning hours of the auction, Seigel received a phone call—somebody had entered a higher bid. Seigel waffled. Did he really want to spend that much money on a baseball card? Seigel's wife, Lorrie, didn't share his ambivalence. "My wife said, 'We have the money to buy it, we have the interest to buy it,'" Seigel remembered. "'You might not ever get this chance again.'"

That was all Seigel needed to hear. He bumped his bid up to $1.1 million; with the buyer's fee, he paid $1.265 million for the Gretzky T206 Wagner.

At a press conference at the California Angels' Edison Field a few days later, Seigel thanked his wife for her support, and she told reporters, "I still can't believe we did it. It was almost like, 'Uh-oh, what did we do?'"

Their thirteen-year-old daughter, Jessica, meanwhile, had her own gripe. "If Dad can spend $1 million on a baseball card," she asked, "why can't I have a horse?"

The world's most famous baseball card sat on a tripod in a jeweler's case in front of the Professional Sports Authenticator booth at the Anaheim Convention Center in the summer of 2006, looking remarkably crisp and fresh for a ninety-six-year-old: no wrinkles, no blemishes, no flabby corners. The borders were so white they looked bleached. The edges appeared straight, and the corners looked sharp enough to draw blood. The black velvet on the display shelf brought out The Card's orange background and the rosy glow in the Flying Dutchman's cheeks. The Gretzky T206 Wagner looked like a million bucks.

Across the hall two other T206 Wagners were on display at the booth for BMW Sportscards, Brian and Michael Wentz's company. Both cards looked stained and worn compared to the Gretzky T206 Wagner—but many collectors still would have eagerly paid an arm

and a leg for them. Brian Seigel had loaned The Card to PSA for display at the twenty-seventh annual National Sports Collectors Convention, and it was one of the stars of the show. A steady stream of
visitors, mostly collectors who had come by the PSA booth to get
cards graded, stopped for a minute or so to catch a closeup of the
most expensive baseball card in the world. Some looked at The Card
with awe and reverence, like visitors to Lourdes. Others shook their
heads in disbelief. "A million dollars for a trimmed card?" one guy
said with a laugh as he walked away.

Card graders, memorabilia dealers, and prominent collectors at
the show were equally divided on the merits of The Card. Some say
there is absolutely no evidence that anything improper has been
done to the Gretzky T206 Wagner. It is an incredible example of a
rare card from the most popular vintage-card set, they argue, an
American icon that would go for $2.35 million when Seigel decided
to sell it. It had held up under the scrutiny of a long line of important collectors who had decided that The Card was worth a fortune.
It has the stamp of approval from PSA, and for many people that is
good enough.

"I believe it is a great card," said Beckett grader Andy Broome. "I
haven't handled it raw, so I don't know firsthand, but I trust PSA's
opinion. Until [it's] proven otherwise, I say this card has not been
doctored."

Others, of course, are more cynical. "Of course it was trimmed,"
one industry executive said. "Did you see how sharp those corners
are? Did you see how white the borders are? It's too good to be
true.

"But even if I magically became the owner of that card I wouldn't
have it looked at again," the executive added. "If it gets the same

grade or better, the fix was in. If they say it was doctored, you make a lot of enemies. No matter what you do, you lose."

The convention center's massive exhibition hall bustled with 700 booths set up by 350 auction houses and dealers, and many brought along binders and boxes full of T206 cards. That's one of the things collectors say is so weird and wonderful about the T206 series: The cards in the set that spawned the rare Gretzky T206 Wagner are ubiquitous. Dealers at the 2006 National offered T206 cards for as low as $60. They're even cheaper on eBay.

"I used to sell T206s to kids—beat-up [cards]—for five dollars. One of the things about the T206 series is that it is so accessible," said Bill Huggins, president of Huggins & Scott Auctions, a Maryland sports-memorabilia business. "They produced so many of these cards. It's easy to start a T206 collection. It's really hard to complete one."

Brian Seigel isn't as much fun as Mike Gidwitz, he's not as flamboyant as Bruce McNall, and he's not as famous as Wayne Gretzky. But for most hobby insiders, he was a capable steward for The Card. Seigel believed that his famous T206 Wagner should be an ambassador for the hobby, a tool to promote trading cards, and soon after he bought it, he tried to mount a tour for The Card, displaying it at every Major League Baseball stadium. But the logistics of a national ballpark tour proved too difficult to overcome. There were insurance questions and conflicts with potential corporate sponsors—noncompete agreements in stadium advertising contracts barred rival soft-drink or beer companies from using the T206 tour as a marketing opportunity—and Seigel's dream died quickly.

Still, Seigel didn't lock the Gretzky T206 Wagner away in a dusty old safe-deposit box. It has been a regular at the annual National Sports Collectors Convention. It was displayed at the Ronald Reagan Presidential Library in Simi Valley, California, in 2003 for a benefit for the Wellness Community, a nonprofit organization that aids cancer patients and their families. It accompanied Collectors Universe chief executive officer Michael Haynes when he rang the bell to open NASDAQ trading on July 22, 2005. And it made one hell of a show-and-tell piece for a sixth-grader named Jeff Lobel. Seigel is Jeff's uncle, and in 2001 Seigel brought the Wagner and other rare and valuable cards to Jeff's class at Westpark Elementary School in Irvine, California.

At least one student thought Seigel was a little crazy for spending $1.265 million on a baseball card. "If I had a million dollars," eleven-year-old Ryan Jones said, "I'd buy a really nice house and two cars." Seigel probably smiled at Ryan's comments, but as a Virginia dealer and collector named Scott Elkins discovered, the Seigels don't tolerate dissent when it comes to their $1.265 million investment. Elkins's experience also shows that there are consequences for people who criticize Bill Mastro's famous discovery. Elkins got into a running battle with Mrs. Seigel on a now-extinct collectors' forum called FullCount.com after Elkins suggested in a posting that the card had been trimmed.

"Board members had been talking about how the card had been trimmed, how it never should have been slabbed in the first place," Elkins said with a laugh. "She came on the board and defended their purchase. She wanted proof that the card had been trimmed. She said I didn't know what I was talking about, and she said the card was not trimmed.

"I referred her to the man who had the before-and-after pictures—

Alan Ray—and I got the feeling she knew I was correct but wanted me to shut up anyway. I finally said, 'It's your money, not mine,' and left it at that.

"I went through a lot of grief after that. I sold everything I had and got out of collecting for a while," Elkins added.

Elkins was easy to dismiss—he is disliked by many people in the hobby. But when veteran T206 collector and dealer Bill Heitman criticized The Card on Network54, people took notice.

In November 2005 a Network54 member named Scott Ingold posted a press release issued by a law firm representing William Miller, a former Collectors Universe executive. Miller had filed a lawsuit that said PSA-DNA, Collectors Universe's autograph-authentication division, had used his name on more than fourteen thousand certificates of authenticity without his permission. The law firm announced that an Orange County, California, jury had ruled in Miller's favor and that the possible awards could total more than $10.5 million. The press release turned out to be wishful thinking on the part of the firm—Miller was eventually awarded just $14,000—but Ingold's post set off a long discussion about the state of the hobby and PSA.

Heitman, the legendary card collector and author of *The Monster*, a well-respected guide to T206 cards, had kept a very low profile in the years before his post. In fact, some hobby veterans had assumed he'd died years earlier. He was, however, very much alive, and his posts in November 2005 gave hobby insiders plenty to talk about for several weeks. Heitman wrote:

When PSA was first starting up, they were practically doing handstands to get to grade the T206 Wagner that McNall and

Gretzky had just bought. I happened to know the pedigree of the card and knew that it had been trimmed. The guy who was going to grade the card stopped by my home on the way to PSA headquarters to grade the card. He knew that the card had been trimmed, but told me PSA had to grade the card because the good publicity that would come from grading the card was all that was important and, besides the card was within the size limitations for T206. I told him that the smaller ones were all American Beauty and he responded that PSA was going to grade the card. I actually talked once to Bruce McNall about this and he acknowledged that he knew the card had been trimmed. So PSA, the owners of the card and the grader of the card knew it was trimmed. But put some plastic over it and all was forgotten.

Some Network54 members were stunned and demanded to know more. "It's not every day that the author of 'THE MONSTER' graces us with his presence!!!" one wrote. "BILL: Please share with us the pedigree of the card!!! PLEASE."

Others scoffed, "PSA says its [sic] real . . . Mastro will say its [sic] real . . . The whole back and forth about the card simply adds to its mystery."

Heitman didn't identify the grader who told him The Card had been trimmed, but his name was already known to many people around the hobby: It was Bill Hughes, the Texas card and comic-book dealer. Hughes freely acknowledged he believed that The Card had been cut from a sheet and trimmed, and he said that was okay with him, even though it violates hobby standards and PSA's own rules. As do many of the people who have invested in or profited from The Card, Hughes minimizes the impact that altering may have had on what has become the ultimate symbol of the hobby.

"I am aware it was part of a strip," he said during a 2005 interview. "We were aware of that when the card came to PSA and I graded the card. This particular card was obviously cut, but if it had been a disgusting card that was cut, of course we would have graded it 'trimmed.' This card was fresh in every way, brand-new looking in every way. . . . Because of the freshness, the great color, the white borders, you know, basically the card looked new. It looked like a card that had come out of a factory and was never packaged, no tobacco stains, nothing wrong with it whatsoever. By virtue of that, the card really warranted being graded as the best example."

Hughes justified ignoring the fact that the card had been altered by saying it had generated a lot of positive publicity for the hobby. "The card is so outstanding, it would have been sacrilegious to call that card trimmed and completely devalue it," he explained. "Just look at what it has done for the hobby."

Hughes admitted that the fact that most T206 Wagners are in poor shape made PSA's deception easier. There really wasn't anything to compare the Gretzky card with. "It would have been a different story if there had been a number of high-grade Wagners in existence at the time," he said.

Hughes's confession didn't shock hobby old-timers. Josh Evans, Bill Mastro's long-standing rival, said Mastro told him several times that he had trimmed the card to make it the best card in the history of the hobby. "The first time he said it, was at a show after it sold for $110,000 to Copeland," Evans remembered. "I said, 'How could you trim a card like that?' He said, 'What's wrong with that? It was over-sized.' I said, 'It doesn't matter. You still have to tell the people who bought it.' It was always an interesting topic of conversation. We also talked about it after Gretzky bought it."

One prominent collector said that the hobby could collapse if it became widely known that The Card violated hobby standards and PSA's own rules. If the hobby's Holy Grail is not as advertised, then where does that leave everyone else's collections? If PSA awarded a high grade to a card its employees knew should have been rejected, then what does that mean for everyone else's cards?

"A lot of collectors would go down," said the hobby insider, who spoke only on condition of anonymity. "PSA would go down. It would be a huge problem for the hobby, and it would be a huge problem for the concept of card grading."

Rumors began swirling in September 2006 that Brian Seigel was entering negotiations to privately sell The Card for between $2.2 and $2.4 million, rumors that Seigel's wife denied. Seigel had stead-fastly turned down offers to sell his famed T206 Wagner—he claimed that Japanese collectors had offered him up to $2 million after a story about The Card aired on television in Japan in 2001—but he finally announced in February 2007 that he had indeed sold the card privately to an anonymous Southern California collector for $2.35 million.

Inside the hobby, some believed that The Card could have sold for more if it had been offered through a public auction, even higher than the $3 million that *Spawn* comic-book creator Todd McFarlane had paid for McGwire's seventieth-home-run ball. But a public auc-tion risked greater public scrutiny, especially with the photographs of the Gretzky T206 Wagner allegedly held by the Wentz brothers and other collectors and the questions about the validity of The Card's PSA 8 rating.

Brian Seigel, like just about every other collector who had owned the Gretzky T206 Wagner, would make his money back and much more. But the future of the world's most famous baseball card would remain cloudy. "All this will come out," said one hobby insider.

For the millions of people who collect baseball cards or autographs or signed bats or jerseys, the issues surrounding the Gretzky T206 Honus Wagner—The Card—probably don't mean lot. It's just a marketing tool to them, a commodity for the snake-oil salesmen and the suckers who are their victims. Whether Michael Gidwitz knew that The Card was trimmed when he bought it—and he freely admits he did—really doesn't mean a thing. Whether Brian Seigel is able to get his money out of it—and more—is irrelevant to a novice collector like Paul Harris, who grew up in Connecticut and on Martha's Vineyard.

His father died before Harris was even a year old, and he grew up idolizing his uncle, Bill Bennett. Uncle Bill was a Brooklyn Dodgers fan, and Harris's first memory is of hearing Vin Scully's voice broadcasting the Dodger game from Los Angeles. Like many baseball fans, Uncle Bill loved to save the cards and balls and the old programs, the mementos of something that is hard to get your arms around, hard, really, to explain at all.

"It was such a big deal," Harris said. "Something that connected us to each other and to the past."

They watched a Dodgers-Yankees World Series together in 1977, the year Reggie Jackson hit three home runs in Game 6 to clinch the series for New York, and Paul did what a million kids have done over the years—he forsook his uncle's team and became a Yankees fan. Harris has two daughters now, and he's given them the same love of baseball and its history that his uncle brought to him, the same connection to the past that Rob Lifson talks about. Harris buys balls signed by Derek Jeter and Reggie Jackson from Major League Baseball's Web site—he doesn't think MLB would sell fraudulent merchandise—and he and his girls gather by the radio in the kitchen of the same summerhouse on Martha's Vineyard and listen to the pop of the bat and the roar of the crowd, just as Harris used to do with Uncle Bill. There are Red Sox fans across the street, and in the mornings there is often a giant box score written in chalk on the pavement, announcing the previous night's winner.

Those are the real collectors, the ones who know they aren't going to sell a baseball card for a million bucks, or hide it in a vault, or trim it to make it look better. These are the fans who carry their love of the game in their hearts, not between slabs of plastic.

Even a businessman as creative and intelligent as Bill Mastro could not have predicted how far this T206 Wagner would go. In the twenty years after Mastro bullied a desperate man in a Hicksville card shop, The Card has become a national icon, in many ways as recognizable as *American Gothic*. It has also become a symbol of a hobby that is out of control.

What does the future hold for The Card? Is it the centerpiece of a creative Ponzi scheme—will somebody eventually get stuck with a worthless piece of antique cardboard while everyone who came before him made a mint?

Or does The Card transcend all that? Does the fact that The Card tramples the rules that govern millions of other baseball cards even really matter? Because when all the hype and the money are removed, it is still a souvenir of a great athlete and another time. It is still a beautiful card.

Even if it is trimmed.

APPENDIX A

TIMELINE

1866 After two years of marriage, Peter and Katheryn Wagner, both twenty-eight years old, leave Prussia for the United States. They settle in the Pittsburgh area, where Peter finds work in western Pennsylvania's coalfields.

Johnannes Peter Wagner—better known as **1874** Honus—is born, the fourth of the Wagners' six children (three others died in infancy).

1897 Honus Wagner makes his National League debut with the Louisville Colonels.

The National League contracts Louisville **1900** and three other clubs, turning the twelve-team league to an eight-city circuit. Colonels owner Barney Dreyfuss buys a share in the Pirates and brings his best players—including Wagner—to Pittsburgh, turning the Bucs into a baseball powerhouse.

1903 ← Pirates win the National League pennant, earn the right to play American League champion Boston in the first World Series. Wagner plays poorly, and Boston wins, five games to three.

Wagner enjoys the best season of his career, ⇢**1908** hits .356 and 109 RBI in 151 games. Pirates blow their chance to force three-way tie for NL pennant with the Cubs and Giants when they lose to Chicago on the last game of the season.

1909 ← Wagner hits .339 and drives in 100 runs in 137 and then leads the Pirates over the American League's Detroit Tigers in seven games, to give Pittsburgh its first World Series title. The American Tobacco Company begins production of baseball cards that would years later be dubbed the T206 set by collector and card scholar Jefferson Burdick. Wagner tells the company he does not want his card distributed in packs of cigarettes and loose tobacco.

Wagner marries longtime girlfriend Bessie Smith. ⇢**1916** The couple eventually has two daughters.

1917 ← After twenty-one years in Major League Baseball, Wagner hangs up his spikes, although he serves the Pirates as a coach for many years after his retirement.

1933← Syracuse factory worker Jefferson Burdick
publishes *The American Card Catalog*, the first attempt to
organize trading cards, and assigns the cards the letters
and numbers they will be known by—*T* stands for "tobacco." The value of most cards listed is under $1; the
T206 Wagner, even then the most expensive card in the
world, is listed at a whopping $50.

Wagner is inducted, with Babe Ruth, Walter →**1936**
Johnson, Christy Mathewson, and Ty Cobb, into the
Baseball Hall of Fame's inaugural class.

1955← Honus Wagner, eighty-one, dies at his home in Carnegie,
Pennsylvania.

Up-and-coming sports-collectibles dealer Bill →**1985**
Mastro buys what is described as a mint T206 Wagner
from collector Alan Ray for $25,000 in a private sale,
beginning an odyssey of ambition, greed, and intrigue
that continues today.

1987← Mastro sells the card to collector Jim Copeland,
the owner of a West Coast sporting-goods
chain, for $110,000.

1991 ↤ Copeland offers the card for auction at Sotheby's; it is
purchased by hockey great Wayne Gretzky and collector/
Los Angeles Kings owner Bruce McNall for $451,000.
Shortly after the auction, the T206 Wagner becomes the
first baseball card to be "graded" by Professional Sports
Authenticator, Inc., which gave it a "PSA NM-MT 8" mark.
The Card is christened the "Gretzky T206 Honus Wagner."

Sold by Gretzky to Wal-Mart and Treat Entertain- ↦*1995*
ment for use as the grand prize in a promotional contest
for $500,000. The Card tours the country in a traveling
memorabilia museum as Wal-Mart tries to reinvigorate the
sagging sale of baseball cards.

1996 ↤ The Gretzky T206 Honus Wagner is won by Patricia Gibbs,
a Florida postal worker, who sells it to pay the taxes she
owes on it. It is auctioned at Christie's (in a sale arranged
by Mastro) for $640,000 to Chicago collector Michael
Gidwitz.

The Card, still known as the Gretzky ↦*2000*
T206 Honus Wagner, is sold by Gidwitz in an eBay
auction arranged by MastroNet Inc. for $1.27 million to
collector Brian Seigel.

2007 ↤ Seigel sells The Card, which he has had reholdered and is
no longer known as the Gretzky T206 Honus Wagner, to
an anonymous collector for $2.35 million.

APPENDIX B

THE MOST VALUABLE BASEBALL CARDS IN THE WORLD

Robert Lifson, president of Robert Edward Auctions, is an expert in the baseball-card and collectibles industry. Lifson has compiled a list of the cards he considers to be among the most valuable in the world (not necessarily in order of value), based on a combination of rarity, auction results, *Sports Market Report* (the Professional Sports Authenticator price guide magazine) value, condition, and his personal opinion based on decades of experience. Assessing the value of a card is subjective, but there are many that are widely recognized by collectors as belonging on any substantial list of the most valuable baseball cards.

Some cards on the list are extremely valuable in any condition, even in the lowest grades. Others are among the most valuable cards in the collecting world only in an extremely high grade, and are of far more modest value in lower grades.

Because of this, the value of a good condition example of some of card collecting's most legendary rare and valuable cards can often be less than the market value of an extremely high-grade example of a relatively common card. He has limited the following list to thirty entries, with a few representing more than just one card. The following list is based on a combination of value and fame in the baseball-card world. The images of these cards, in most cases, have been reproduced in print so many times that they have literally been engrained into the collective consciousness of collectors. These classic high-profile cards play a role in defining the market for all vintage baseball cards.

Following the list are additional notes regarding extremely valuable cards that are not listed simply because they are not commercially well known, and how the impact of condition on value can vary dramatically with different cards and sets.

KEY

PSA — Professional Sports Authenticator

GAI — Global Authentication, Inc.

SMR — *Sports Market Report*

SGC — Sportscard Guaranty

MT — Mint

NM — Near Mint

EX — Excellent

VG — Very good

GD — Good

FR — Fair

PR — Poor

1. T206 Honus Wagner: Universally recognized as the most valuable of all baseball cards. Even in lowest grade PSA 1 FR-GD, this card would sell for well over $100,000. In December 2004, a PSA PR-FR 1 sold for $101,414. A different PSA 1 Wagner sold for $109,638 in 2004 and yet another PSA 1 sold for $132,000 in 2005. In 2005, a PSA GOOD 2 sold for $236,705. A GAI 3.5 VG+ (now in an SGC 30 Good holder) sold for $456,057 in December

2005. A PSA GOOD 2 sold in December 2006 for $294,337.

2. 1914 Baltimore News Babe Ruth "Rookie Card": Only about ten are known to exist. With the exception of a very few super high-grade high-demand commercial cards (a 1952 Topps Mantle in Gem Mint would sell for hundreds of thousands of dollars), this is arguably second in value only to a T206 Wagner. In 2005, a PSA VG-EX 4 example sold for $243,000, and in 2006, a PSA PR-FR 1 example sold for $150,800.

3. T206 Eddie Plank: This card is more common than Wagner's but is historically one of the most valuable of all cards. A PSA 7 sold for $93, 000 in 2003 and PSA 8 sold for $203,000 in 1999. There have been many, many sales in VG up to EX in the $30,000, $40,000, $50,000 range.

4. T206 Joe Doyle NY Nat'l: A rare variation sold in August 2000 for $178,598. A T206 Doyle—PSA 3—sold in April 2003 for $64,100 (a thin market; not everyone wants this card, but there are only a few known).

5. T206 Magie: A rare error card that spells Philadelphia outfielder Sherry Magee's name with an "ie" at the end. The error was corrected and examples with the incorrect spelling are very rare. This may seem to be a minor error, but because this card is part of the T206 series, the most popular set of the 1910 era, it has always been a highly sought after and extremely valuable card. Lists for $55,000 in

SMR in PSA NM-MT 8, would probably sell for much more. A PSA VG-EX 4 sold at auction in 2006 for $19,720.

6. T206 Ty Cobb with Ty Cobb Back. Once again a great rarity of special interest to T206 collectors. Traditionally thought of as one of the most valuable vintage cards, it has lost a little favor in recent years—one sold for $36,099 in July 2000. Approximately twelve are known to exist. A find of five examples sold at auction individually in 1997, all at the same time, yielded the following results: VG-EX $32,598; VG/EX (stain back) $22,224; GOOD+ $24,650; GOOD $22,425; GOOD (pencil marks on back) $18,522. The lowest grade of these five cards, the example with writing on the reverse and which sold for $18,522 in 1997, was offered at auction again in 2005, selling for $29,000.

7. T210 Old Mill Tobacco Joe Jackson: Six years ago it was worth less than $10,000, but in April 2005 it exploded in value, selling for $92,800 in an REA auction. That example was encapsulated "Authentic" by PSA but was assigned no numerical grade due to unusual borders. A second example at Mastro Auctions graded PSA 5 MK (MK=mark on back due to stain) sold for $112,000. A third example, graded VG by SGC, set a new record of $116,000 in an REA auction in April 2006. Collectors have a special appreciation for rare cards, as well as cards of Joe Jackson, of which there are few. This card is now universally recognized as one of the most valuable cards among vintage-card collectors.

8. 1887 N172 Old Judge Cap Anson in street clothes: This is the "Honus Wagner" of pre-1900 cards. Value: In excellent condition, worth much more than $100,000. This is a very famous card, it is from the most important nineteenth-century set, and there are only three or four in existence. Universally accepted as one of the best of all cards but so rare and in such strong hands that it has not come up for auction in many years. (Last sold for about $60,000 many years ago and the card has many more collectors interested in it now.)

9. 1933 Goudey Gum #106 Nap Lajoie: Traditionally known as one of the most valuable of all cards. In the "old days" it was known as one of the "Big 3" cards, referring to Wagner, Plank, and Lajoie. In Excellent condition, it is worth $20,000. There are a lot of these but not too many in holders with high numbers, so in PSA 8 or better it is much more valuable. SMR is $50,000 in PSA NM-MT 8, but worth $100,000+ in PSA MINT 9. Two examples in PSA MINT 9 have been sold at auction in 2006 for $141,280 and $123,488.

10. E90-1 American Caramel Joe Jackson: Now considered one of the classic most valuable vintage cards. This is a very famous card, really is Joe Jackson's undisputed rookie, and is a very rare card in the set that is the "T206 of caramel cards." Value: Though usually not found in high grade—that's how caramel cards are—in excellent condition it would be over $50,000; in lower grades, over $10,000.

11. T205 Gold Border Ty Cobb: "Condition high value card"—
    SMR lists VG-EX 4 at $1,900 (which is low for a good-
    looking VG-EX), $12,000 in PSA 7, $72,500 in PSA NM-MT
    8, and $100,000 for PSA 9 (this is just a theoretical SMR list
    price; no T205 Ty Cobb has ever been graded PSA MINT 9).

12. All four T206 Cobbs: There are four cards of Ty Cobb in
    the T206 "White-Border" tobacco card set. With reference
    to value, all four are similar to the T205 Gold Border of Ty
    Cobb as far as being "condition high value cards." There
    are many more valuable cards in circulated condition, but
    few more valuable in the highest grades. Example: T206 Ty
    Cobb Green Background PSA VG-EX 4 lists for $3,800.
    PSA MINT 9 lists for $70,000.

13. In the classic T205 and T206 tobacco card sets, there are
    "condition high value cards" (similar to Ty Cobb in the mar-
    ket's current approach to value) in each set for a few key Hall
    of Famers (such as Walter Johnson and Christy Mathewson).
    For example, a T206 Walter Johnson portrait pose in VG-EX
    is worth between $500 and $800. The same card graded PSA
    NM-MT 8 sold at auction in 2005 for $37,700.

14. T3 Turkey Red Ty Cobb: Recognized as an extremely valuable
    classic, a PSA 8 sold for $92,160 in 2005. All of the big stars in
    the set, as is the case in all of the most popular and classic
    card issues, are extremely valuable in the highest grades.

15a. and 15b. 1915 Cracker Jacks: Ty Cobb (SMR in 8 = $25,000,
    in 9 = $75,000) and Joe Jackson (SMR in 8 = $38,500, in

9=$85,000). Cracker Jacks are among the most popular of all vintage cards. Other stars in this set are also extremely valuable in high grade.

16a. and 16b. 1914 Cracker Jacks: Ty Cobb (SMR in 8=$26,500, SMR in 9=$60,000) and Joe Jackson (SMR in 8=$40,000, in 9=$80,000. (1915 Cracker Jacks are very similar to 1914, but 1914s are rarer, especially in high grade). A 1914 Cracker Jack of Ty Cobb graded NM-MT 8 by PSA sold at auction for $61,809 in November 2006.

17. 1914 Cracker Jack Christy Mathewson: This is one of the extremely valuable vintage classics. The pose of the 1914 Mathewson card is different from the pose on the 1915 card, and has come to be recognized by collectors as one of the key cards among all Cracker Jacks. SMR in PSA 9 grade=$95,000. PSA VG-EX 4 sold at an REA auction in 2006 for $40,600.

18. 1916 M101-4 and M101-5 "Sporting News" Babe Ruth: This very famous card is Ruth's first card as a Major Leaguer, so it is often called his rookie card (even though a 1914 Baltimore News card was issued two years earlier that features Ruth with Baltimore in the Minor Leagues). In PSA 4=$10,000+, in PSA 5=$15,000+, in PSA 6=$20,000+, in PSA 8=$100,000. One of the classic cards collectors seem to gravitate to; while rare, it is actually possible to obtain.

19. 1932 US Caramel Lindy Linstrom: Only two or three are known, and in 1999 one sold for $92,000. This card got a

lot of publicity for being offered for a million dollars many years ago, which may have helped its value. Not a high demand card, but it is really rare, and if it went up for auction would probably sell for a similar price.

20. All four 1933 Goudey Ruths and both 1933 Goudey Gehrigs: There are four cards of Babe Ruth and two of Lou Gehrig in the 1933 Goudey Gum set. All are "high value condition cards." Typical is #53 Ruth, which lists for $5,750 in PSA EX 5, $14,500 in NM-MT PSA 7, $40,000 in PSA 8, and $105,000 in PSA 9.

21. 1934 Goudey Lou Gehrig: There are two poses of Lou Gehrig in the 1933 Goudey Gum set. Both poses, the portrait especially, are "high value condition cards." The #61 Gehrig batting pose lists in SMR for $50,000 in PSA MINT 9. The #37 Gehrig portrait pose lists in SMR for $75,000 in PSA MINT 9. Both cards are worth between $2,500 and $4,000 in EX-MT condition.

22. 1951 Bowman Mantle: Big-time classic rookie card and extraordinarily valuable in PSA MINT 9 or PSA GEM-MT 10. Estimate: PSA MINT 9 would sell for well over $50,000. PSA GEM-MT 10 would sell for well over $100,000.

23. 1952 Topps Mantle: Big-time classic and extraordinarily valuable in PSA MINT 9 or PSA GEM-MT 10. A PSA MINT 9 sold at auction in December 2006 reportedly sold for $282,587. The December SMR value listed for this card was $135,000. A PSA GEM-MT 10 of this card (only four exam-

ples have ever been graded GEM-MT 10) would presumably sell for considerably more. The 1952 Topps Mickey Mantle is one of card collecting's most famous cards. It is very valuable in any condition. There are hundreds of examples known but the demand is always extremely high. In lower grades this card is still worth thousands of dollars, but is considerably more affordable. Many examples in conditions ranging from Good to Excellent sell each year, at levels ranging between $2,500 and $10,000 depending on overall eye-appeal and the exact condition of the card.

24. 1952 Bowman, 1953 Bowman, and especially 1953 Topps Mickey Mantles: All worth big money in PSA 9 and 10, as above 1952 Topps Mantle. All "high-value condition cards." All relatively affordable in lower grades and not particularly rare, but extremely valuable in mint or gem mint condition. A 1952 Bowman #101 Mickey Mantle graded GEM-MT 10 by PSA sold at auction for $43,125 in 2004.

25. 1949 Leaf Gum—Satchel Paige: Really rare and extremely valuable in high grade. Lists for $85,000 in PSA 9.

26. 1952 Topps #1 Andy Pafko: Worth $25 in GD condition but sold for $83,000 in PSA MINT 10. Such #1 cards in general are "condition rarities" because they tend to gravitate to the top of stacks of cards and are therefore subject to more wear than other cards. The #1 cards from the most popular sets, therefore, tend to sell for a significant premium to collectors putting together high-grade complete

sets. The #1 Andy Pafko in 1952 Topps and the #1 Benny Bengough in the 1933 Goudey set are the most famous and valuable of these #1 card "condition rarities." It is ironic that the #1 card in many sets is currently so valuable in extremely high grade, as these cards are rarely the biggest stars, and are of interest only to high-grade set collectors. These cards have the potential to be extremely volatile in value. An $83,000 card today can easily become a $10,000 card tomorrow. The 1933 Goudey #1 Benny Bengough, worth approximately $100 in GD condition, lists for $80,000 in PSA MINT 9.

27. 1933 Goudey "Sport King" Babe Ruth: One of the most famous and recognizable high-value 1930s cards—but only sells for a super high value in super high grade—$100,000 SMR listed value in MINT 9. Many sales in the $20,000 range in PSA NM-MT 8. This is one of Babe Ruth's most classic cards.

28. 1939, 1940, and 1941 Play Ball Gum Inc. Ted Williams and Joe DiMaggio in all three sets, and 1940 Play Ball Joe Jackson: All are "high-value condition cards." Reported auction sales include: 1939 Play Ball MINT 9 #92 Ted Williams, $71,588; 1940 Play Ball #27 Ted Williams PSA GEM-MT 10, $79,410 in 2004; 1941 Play Ball #72 Joe DiMaggio PSA MINT 9, $96,074 in 2004, and 1941 Play Ball PSA MINT 9, $65,493 in 2005.

29. 1954 Topps Hank Aaron: Classic rookie card of Hank Aaron. It is very famous, not particularly rare, and avail-

able at very affordable levels ($300 to $1,000) in grades ranging from GD to EX, but has sold for extremely high levels in the highest grades. Reported sales for $110,000 and $90,199 in PSA GEM-MT 10 in 2004. Many sales in $15,000 to $20,000 range in PSA MINT 9.

30. 1951 Bowman Willie Mays rookie: One sold for $109,639 in PSA 9 in 2001. This card has always been far less sought-after than Mickey Mantle's rookie card from the same set and this isolated sale at $109,639 may not be indicative of current market value. The current SMR list price on this card is $55,000. When this card sold for $109,639, it was the only example graded MINT 9 by PSA. As of December 2006 there are seven examples graded by PSA at this level. This fact, combined with the relative lack of enthusiasm for Willie Mays cards in general by collectors (compared to cards of Mickey Mantle from the same sets), makes this card far less valuable than suggested by the 2001 auction sale. This card is still one of the classic postwar rookie cards and one of the most valuable of all 1950s baseball cards.

There are many esoteric, unique, or almost unique cards, many pre-1900, that have or would sell, if offered, for $50,000 or $100,000 or more, but they are so rare, so "not commercial," and not universally recognized that they don't belong on a list of the world's most famous and valuable baseball cards.

Examples include: 1886–1890 Old Judge cigarette cards of Pacific Coast League players (these are very obscure and extremely rare cards that would sell for $50,000 to $100,000 or more, regardless of condition, if available). There are a number of circa 1886 Kalamazoo

Bats, mostly Hall of Famers, that would sell for $50,000 or more if available, and several have, in fact, sold for $50,000 to $75,000 (and more) privately. The same goes for Hall of Famer 1886 Four Base Hits tobacco cards (only two examples of Mike "King" Kelly are known from this set; each would easily sell for $100,000 or more); 1886 N167 Old Judge cards have sold for $40,000 and more at auction.

Extremely exotic rarities may sometimes sell for sums that rival (or exceed) the commercially famous classic cards listed above. As noted, some of the cards would be among the most valuable of all cards in *any* grade—among them are the T206 Wagner and the 1914 Baltimore News Ruth. Others might be worth thousands in any grade but are not extremely rare and are among the most valuable of all cards only in extremely high grade.

The "slope" of value plotted against grades is different for really rare cards than for more common cards. A relatively common but always sought-after 1952 Topps Mickey Mantle might be worth $1,000 to $2,000 in PSA 1 (depending on visual appeal), $5,000 in VG, and $150,000+ in PSA MINT 9, while a 1914 Babe Ruth rookie is valued at well over $100,000 in PSA PR-FR 1. A PSA VG-EX 4 Ruth rookie sold for $243,000 in 2005. If a PSA EX 5 came up it would probably sell for around $300,000 to $400,000, and if a PSA 7 or PSA 8 came up (none are known to exist in this high grade) it would probably sell for between $500,000 and $1 million. But not millions. The curve is much flatter on an extremely rare card such as the 1914 Baltimore News Ruth than with the 1952 Topps Mantle. There are hundreds of 1952 Topps Mickey Mantles. According to the PSA population reports (which provides a record of how many of each card have been graded and in what condition), an incredible 763 Mantle cards from 1952 Topps have been graded by PSA as of December 2006. Hundreds of additional 1952 Topps Mickey Mantle cards exist that have never been submitted for grading to PSA, or have been graded by other services. In comparison, there are only about ten 1914 Babe Ruth Baltimore News rookie cards in existence. The general rule of thumb is, the more common the card, the greater the premium in terms of percentage for the highest graded examples. The rarer the card, the less an impact condition has on value. Similarly, the higher the value in "circulated" condition (and, understandably, value is often related to rarity), the less of an increase in value in terms of percentage is awarded for examples in the highest grades. If a card is worth $100,000 in GD condition, it is already extremely valuable and it is more difficult for it to sell for a large multiple in higher grade. This $100,000 card is not going to sell for two hundred times this sum (which would be $20 million) in MINT condition. But if a card is worth approximately $500 in GD condition, as is the case with a 1933 Goudey #53 Babe Ruth, the lower value in lower grade allows for a much greater multiple of the GOOD value in higher grade. The 1933 Goudey #53 Ruth lists in SMR for $40,000 (80×$500) in NM-MT condition, and $105,000 (210×$500) in MINT condition.

NOTES

PROLOGUE

2 *Lifson even proclaimed:* "Wagner Card Set for a $1M At-Bat," Owen
Moritz, *Daily News* (New York), June 7, 2000.

2 *Some people say that Wagner:* "The Wagner Is in a League by Itself,"
Van Nightingale, *Los Angeles Times*, July 7, 1991.

2 *Only a few dozen:* "Much Valued Then, Worth a Mint Now,"
Dwight Chapin, *San Francisco Chronicle*, September 4, 2003.

3 *The current owner:* "Wagner's Wild Card: Mystery Has Surrounded
Honus T206 Since 1909," Michael O'Keeffe and Bill Madden,
Daily News (New York), March 25, 2001.

3 *The Gretzky T206 Wagner:* "Baseball's Card of Cards Is Up for
Grabs," Alexandra Peers, *Wall Street Journal*, September 20,
1996.

3 *It has been the headliner:* "Famous Wagner Card Accompanies
Collectors Universe CEO to NASDAQ Opening," Collectors
Universe.com, July 22, 2005.

4 *During that summer of 2000:* "Holy Grail: The Honus Wagner
T206," Brian Kates, *Daily News* (New York), June 22, 2003.

5 *He introduced me to his staff:* Stephen Wong, *Smithsonian Baseball: Inside the World's Finest Private Collections* (New York: Harper-Collins, 2005).

CHAPTER 1: EXPRESSWAY TO FORTUNE

10 *Ray also had another rare:* "Wagner's Wild Card: Mystery Has Surrounded Honus T206 Since 1909," Michael O'Keeffe and Bill Madden, *Daily News* (New York), March 25, 2001.

10 *Mastro had been a fixture:* Stephen Wong, *Smithsonian Baseball: Inside the World's Finest Private Collections* (New York: Harper-Collins, 2005). Also see "Take Me Out to the Sports Memorabilia Dealer," Judd Tully, *Cigar Aficionado*, May/June 2001; "Bill Mastro—The Ringmaster of Memorabilia," David Laurell, *Sports Market Report*, October 2005; and "My Mentor Frank Nagy," Bill Mastro, MastroNet.com, December 2005.

12 *Mastro had seen millions of cards:* "Wagner's Wild Card: Mystery Has Surrounded Honus T206 Since 1909," Michael O'Keeffe and Bill Madden.

14 *Halper, the New Jersey businessman:* "Commentary: Super-Fan's Collection Was Spurred by Love, Not Greed," David Goodwillie, Newhouse News Service, January 11, 2006. Also see "A $1 Million Honus?" Doris Athineos, *Forbes*, November 4, 1996; "Sotheby's Begins Baseball Auction," Hal Bock, Associated Press, September 23, 1999; "Chew on This: $7,475 Paid for Cobb's Dentures," Hal Bock, Associated Press, September 28 1999; "Crystal Clear, No Comedy: Mantle's Glove Worth $239,000," Elliott Harris, *Chicago Sun-Times*, September 29, 1999; "This Auction Brings Out the Crazy Money," Rich Hoffmann, *Philadelphia Daily News*, September 30, 1999; "PSA1

Wagner Sold for a Record Price of $110K," T206Museum.com, May 2004; and "T206 Wagner PSA-2 Sold for a Record Price of $236,706," T206Museum.com, April 2005.

14 *There may never be another collector:* "Halper, Renowned Collector, Dies; Yank Partner Kept 'Cooperstown South,'" Bill Madden, *Daily News* (New York), December 19, 2005.

15 *At the 1994 press conference to announce:* "Halper, Renowned Collector, Dies; Yank Partner Kept 'Cooperstown South,'" Bill Madden, *Daily News* (New York), December 19, 2005.

15 *The bulk of the Halper collection:* "Cooperstown Halls Off Halper Collection," Bill Madden, *Daily News* (New York), September 2, 1999. Also see "Baseball Collector Halper Dies," Associated Press, December 19, 2005.

15 *In September 2006, Lifson would auction thirty balls:* "Pete's Sign of His Sorry Times," Michael O'Keeffe and Teri Thompson, *Daily News* (New York), September 18, 2006. Also see "$30G for Pete's Ball Haul," Michael O'Keeffe, *Daily News* (New York), September 22, 2006.

15 *The Halper auction remains:* "Going, Going, Gone: The Halper Collection Auction Was a Grand Slam," Josh Elliot, *Sports Illustrated*, October 4, 1999.

15 *"It really doesn't get any better":* "Industry Expert: Meet the Man Behind the Famous Barry Halper Auction," *Beckett Sports Collectibles*, May 2004.

CHAPTER 2: KING OF THE HILL

17 *The card's skyrocketing price tag:* "Wagner's Wild Card: Mystery Has Surrounded Honus T206 Since 1909," Michael O'Keeffe and Bill Madden, *Daily News* (New York), March 25, 2001.

17 *In many ways he is the George Steinbrenner*: "Bill Mastro—The Ringmaster of Memorabilia," David Laurell, *Sports Market Report*, October 2005. Also see "What's in These Cards Is in the Genes," Ron Grossman, *Chicago Tribune*, February 1, 1990; and "Take Me Out to the Sports Memorabilia Dealer," Judd Tully, *Cigar Aficionado*, May/June 2001.

17 *The auction house he founded, Mastro Auctions:* "Flip Taking Control of Online Auction House," Lee Murphy, *Crain's Chicago Business*, January 31, 2005.

18 *"The others are all dinosaurs"*: "Mastro Nets Big Slice of Market," Danielle Arnet, *Maine Antique Digest*, September 2003.

18 *In recent years Mastro Auctions has even expanded:* "Flip Taking Control of Online Auction House," Lee Murphy, *Crain's Chicago Business*, January 31, 2005.

18 *When Mastro began his business*: "Bill Mastro—The Ringmaster of Memorabilia," David Laurell, *Sports Market Report*, October 2005. Also see "Opinion: A King-Sized Auction of Sports Memorabilia," Bill Wallace, *Bridge News*, April 27, 1999.

18 *Back then, in the mid-1960s:* Stephen Wong, *Smithsonian Baseball: Inside the World's Finest Private Collections* (New York: Harper-Collins, 2005). Also see "Take Me Out to the Sports Memorabilia Dealer," Judd Tully, *Cigar Aficionado*, May/June 2001; "Bill Mastro—The Ringmaster of Memorabilia," David Laurell, *Sports Market Report*, October 2005 and "My Mentor Frank Nagy," Bill Mastro, MastroNet.com, December 2005.

19 *Bill Mastro helped change all that*: "Mastro Makes Move Online," Gregory Lewis and Dwight Chapin, *San Francisco Chronicle*, June 3, 2000. Also see "Going, Going . . . Mastro Fine Sports of Oak

Brook Takes Online Auctions to Another Level," *Chicago Daily Herald*, April 26, 1999.

20 *Mastro sold his auction house in late 2004*: "Flip Taking Control of Online Auction House," Lee Murphy, *Crain's Chicago Business*, January 31, 2005. Also see "Flip: The Latest Chapter in the Filipowski Tale," Terry Savage, *Chicago Sun-Times*, August 20, 2006.

20 *"I'm not like some other executives"*: "Bill Mastro—The Ringmaster of Memorabilia," David Laurell, *Sports Market Report*, October 2005.

21 *Professional Sports Authenticator, a division of a company:* "Making the Grades," Diana Bosetti, *Orange County Business Journal*, February 3, 1997. Also see "Collectors Switch to Slab to Improve Cards' Value," Reid Creager, *Detroit Free Press*, March 3, 1999; and "On the Road: Grading Baseball Cards," *Inc.*, April 1, 1999; and "The Who's Who of Card Grading," Henry Woodruff, TradingCardCentral.com, August 9, 2004, Annual Report, Collectors Universe, 2005.

21 *A few months after Brian Seigel paid $1.265 million:* "PSA-1 Wagner Sold for Record Price Once Again," T206Museum.com, January 2002.

22 *As the value of cards skyrocketed in the 1980s:* "Making the Grades," Diana Bosetti, *Orange County Business Journal*, February 3, 1997. Also see "Collectors Switch to Slab to Improve Cards' Value," Reid Creager, *Detroit Free Press*, March 3, 1999; and "On the Road: Grading Baseball Cards," *Inc.*, April 1, 1999.

25 *Jim Copeland, the well-heeled owner:* "Wagner's Wild Card: Mystery Has Surrounded Honus T206 Since 1909," Michael O'Keeffe and Bill Madden, *Daily News*, March 25, 2001.

CHAPTER 3: TOBACCO ROAD

29 *In 1910 an astounding 10 billion cigarettes:* Scot A. Reader, *Inside T206: A Collectors Guide to the Classic Baseball Card Set* (self-published, 2006).

29 *The T206 series is so much bigger:* Bill Heitman, *The Monster* (Laurel, Md.: Den Collector's Den, 1980), and Stephen Wong, *Smithsonian Baseball: Inside the World's Finest Private Collections* (New York: HarperCollins, 2005).

29 *Baseball historian Hank Thomas and his partners Frank Ceresi and Kevin Keating:* "Quite the Card," Michael O'Keeffe, *Daily News* (New York), October 16, 2005.

30 *As baseball became an increasingly important part:* Pete Williams, *Card Sharks: How Upper Deck Turned a Child's Hobby into a High-Stakes, Billion-Dollar Business* (New York: Macmillan, 1995). Also see David Rudd Cycleback, "A Brief History of Baseball Cards," Cycleback.com; David Plaut, *Start Collecting Baseball Cards* (Philadelphia: Running Press, 1989); and Stephen Wong, *Smithsonian Baseball: Inside the World's Finest Private Collections* (New York: HarperCollins, 2005).

30 *Unlike modern cards, these cards:* RobertEdwardAuctions.com, April 2006 Auction Catalogue; and Pete Williams, *Card Sharks: How Upper Deck Turned a Child's Hobby into a High-Stakes, Billion-Dollar Business* (New York: Macmillan, 1995). David Rudd Cycleback, "A Brief History of Baseball Cards," Cycleback.com.

31 *The first baseball cards modern fans would recognize:* Pete Williams, *Card Sharks: How Upper Deck Turned a Child's Hobby into a High-Stakes, Billion-Dollar Business* (New York: Macmillan, 1995).

32 *Then the American Tobacco Company came along*: Scot A. Reader, *Inside T206: A Collectors Guide to the Classic Baseball Card Set* (self-published, 2006). Also see Pete Williams, *Card Sharks: How Upper Deck Turned a Child's Hobby into a High-Stakes, Billion-Dollar Business* (New York: Macmillan, 1995); and Bill Heitman, *The Monster* (Laurel, Md.: Den Collector's Den, 1980).

33 *The T206 series has always been popular*: Scot A. Reader, *Inside T206: A Collectors Guide to the Classic Baseball Card Set* (self-published, 2006); and Bill Heitman, *The Monster* (Laurel, Md.: Den Collector's Den, 1980). Also see Stephen Wong, *Smithsonian Baseball: Inside the World's Finest Private Collections* (New York: HarperCollins, 2005).

33 *Most of the studio portraits*: Scot A. Reader, *Inside T206: A Collectors Guide to the Classic Baseball Card Set* (self-published, 2006). Also see "Honus Wagner Original T206 Pose Carl Horner Photograph sold for $18,650," T206Museum.com, April 2005.

33 *The cards were printed*: Scot A. Reader, *Inside T206: A Collectors Guide to the Classic Baseball Card Set* (self-published, 2006), and Bill Heitman, *The Monster* (Laurel, Md.: Den Collector's Den, 1980).

34 *Based on a 1915 U.S. government report*: Scot A. Reader, *Inside T206: A Collectors Guide to the Classic Baseball Card Set* (self-published, 2006).

34 *The T206 Wagner isn't the only*: Scot A. Reader, *Inside T206: A Collectors Guide to the Classic Baseball Card Set* (self-published, 2006); and Bill Heitman, *The Monster* (Laurel, Md.: Den Collector's Den, 1980). Also see Stephen Wong, *Smithsonian Baseball: Inside the World's Finest Private Collections* (New York: HarperCollins, 2005).

35 *Honus Wagner was at the peak of his career*: Dennis DeValeria and Jeanne Burke DeValeria, *Honus Wagner: A Biography* (New York: Henry Holt, 1996). Also see "Honus Wagner," Jan Finkel, Bioproj.SABR.org, and William Hageman, *Honus: The Life and Times of a Baseball Hero* (Champaign, Ill.: Sagamore, 1996).

36 *By 1910, Wagner's likeness*: Dennis DeValeria and Jeanne Burke DeValeria, *Honus Wagner: A Biography* (New York: Henry Holt, 1996).

36 *But Wagner reacted swiftly and surely*: Dennis DeValeria and Jeanne Burke DeValeria, *Honus Wagner: A Biography* (New York: Henry Holt, 1996). Also see Stephen Wong, *Smithsonian Baseball: Inside the World's Finest Private Collections* (New York: HarperCollins, 2005); Scot A. Reader, *Inside T206: A Collectors Guide to the Classic Baseball Card Set* (self-published, 2006); Bill Heitman, *The Monster* (Laurel, Md.: Den Collector's Den, 1980).

37 *Another reason that Olbermann and his allies*: Dennis DeValeria and Jeanne Burke DeValeria, *Honus Wagner: A Biography* (New York: Henry Holt, 1996).

38 *There is, however, one serious flaw*: Dennis DeValeria and Jeanne Burke DeValeria, *Honus Wagner: A Biography* (New York: Henry Holt, 1996).

38 *By 1909, Wagner, the son of a coal-mining immigrant*: Dennis DeValeria and Jeanne Burke DeValeria, *Honus Wagner: A Biography* (New York: Henry Holt, 1996). Also see "Honus Wagner," Jan Finkel, Bioproj.SABR.org, and William Hageman, *Honus: The Life and Times of a Baseball Hero* (Champaign, Ill.: Sagamore, 1996).

38 *Wagner, in other words, was a respectable man*: Dennis DeValeria
    and Jeanne Burke DeValeria, *Honus Wagner: A Biography* (New
    York: Henry Holt, 1996).

39 *"A belief in their deleterious effects"*: "Legal Wheels Grind Back to
    Smoking," David G. Savage, *Los Angeles Times*, December 16, 1999.

39 *In addition, the two men most responsible*: Dennis DeValeria and
    Jeanne Burke DeValeria, *Honus Wagner: A Biography* (New York:
    Henry Holt, 1996).

39 *The Wagner T206, Scot Reader added*: Scot A. Reader, *Inside T206:
    A Collectors Guide to the Classic Baseball Card Set* (self-published,
    2006).

40 *Other tobacco-card sets were issued*: David Plaut, *Start Collecting
    Baseball Cards* (Phildadelphia: Running Press, 1989). Also see
    Stephen Wong, *Smithsonian Baseball: Inside the World's Finest
    Private Collections* (New York: HarperCollins, 2005); Pete
    Williams, *Card Sharks: How Upper Deck Turned a Child's Hobby
    into a High-Stakes, Billion-Dollar Business* (New York: Macmillan,
    1995); "A Brief History of Baseball Cards," David Rudd Cycle-
    back, Cycleback.com; "Tobacco Baseball Cards and Wagner's
    Own Wagner Card," Frank Ceresi, BaseballAlmanac.com.

41 *One development in the Jazz Age*: Pete Williams, *Card Sharks: How
    Upper Deck Turned a Child's Hobby into a High-Stakes, Billion-
    Dollar Business* (New York: Macmillan, 1995).

41 *The first commercially successful bubble gum*: Pete Williams, *Card
    Sharks: How Upper Deck Turned a Child's Hobby into a High-Stakes,
    Billion-Dollar Business* (New York: Macmillan, 1995); and David
    Plaut, *Start Collecting Baseball Cards* (Phildadelphia: Running
    Press, 1989).

42 *Meanwhile there was a factory worker from Syracuse:* "One of a Kind Collection: Obscure Syracuse Electrician, a Card Pioneer, Gets His Due," Sean Kirst, *Syracuse Post-Standard*, June 30, 1993; "The King of Card Collectors Has No Statistics on His Grave," Sean Kirst, *Syracuse Post-Standard*, August 1, 1997; "Decades Later, a Friendship Has Been Chiseled in Stone," Sean Kirst, *Syracuse Post-Standard*, November 14, 1997. Also see "Another Look at the Burdick Collection," George Vrechek, OldBaseball.com.

43 *"All he was interested in was cards":* "Decades Later, a Friendship Has Been Chiseled in Stone," Sean Kirst, *Syracuse Post-Standard*, November 14, 1997.

43 *As in World War I, World War II paper and cardboard:* Pete Williams, *Card Sharks: How Upper Deck Turned a Child's Hobby into a High-Stakes, Billion-Dollar Business* (New York: Macmillan, 1995).

CHAPTER 4: A WHOLE NEW STRATOSPHERE

45 *Jim Copeland paid over 400 percent:* "Wagner's Wild Card: Mystery Has Surrounded Honus T206 Since 1909," Michael O'Keeffe and Bill Madden, *Daily News* (New York), March 25, 2001.

45 *Copeland decided to sell his entire 873-piece collection:* "The Wagner Is in a League by Itself," Van Nightingale, *Los Angeles Times*, July 7, 1991.

45 *Sotheby's had resisted jumping:* "Baseball's Card of Cards Is Up for Grabs," Alexandra Peers, *Wall Street Journal*, September 20, 1996.

46 *Rumors were also beginning to circulate:* "Baseball's Card of Cards Is Up for Grabs," Alexandra Peers, *Wall Street Journal*, September 20, 1996.

46 *About eight hundred of the hobby's wealthies collectors:* Pete Williams, *Card Sharks: How Upper Deck Turned a Child's Hobby into a*

High-Stakes, Billion-Dollar Business (New York: Macmillan, 1995).

48 *"Really, that was the first auction"*: "Take Me Out to the Sports Memorabilia Dealer," Judd Tully, *Cigar Aficionado*, May/June 2001.

CHAPTER 5: THE FLYING DUTCHMAN

50 *Honus Wagner was an eight-time National League batting champion*: Dennis DeValeria and Jeanne Burke DeValeria, *Honus Wagner: A Biography* (New York: Henry Holt, 1996). Also see "Honus Wagner," Jan Finkel, Bioproj.SABR.org; V. Robert Agostino, *A Track Through Time: A Centennial History of Carnegie, Pennsylvania* (Pittsburgh: Wolfson, 1994); and William Hageman, *Honus: The Life and Times of a Baseball Hero* (Champaign, Ill.: Sagamore, 1996).

51 *Many students of baseball history*: Dennis DeValeria and Jeanne Burke DeValeria, *Honus Wagner: A Biography* (New York: Henry Holt, 1996). Also see William Hageman, *Honus: The Life and Times of a Baseball Hero* (Champaign, Ill.: Sagamore, 1996).

53 *When the American League declared itself*: Dennis DeValeria and Jeanne Burke DeValeria, *Honus Wagner: A Biography* (New York: Henry Holt, 1996).

53 *Wagner's highest honor came in 1936*: Dennis DeValeria and Jeanne Burke DeValeria, *Honus Wagner: A Biography* (New York: Henry Holt, 1996); and William Hageman, *Honus: The Life and Times of a Baseball Hero* (Champaign, Ill.: Sagamore, 1996).

55 *"He wasn't just the greatest"*: Dennis DeValeria and Jeanne Burke DeValeria, *Honus Wagner: A Biography* (New York: Henry Holt, 1996).

55 *John Peter Wagner—Honus is a diminutive:* Dennis DeValeria and Jeanne Burke DeValeria, *Honus Wagner: A Biography* (New York: Henry Holt, 1996); and William Hageman, *Honus: The Life and Times of a Baseball Hero* (Champaign, Ill.: Sagamore, 1996).

57 *The Wagner brothers picked up:* Dennis DeValeria and Jeanne Burke DeValeria, *Honus Wagner: A Biography* (New York: Henry Holt, 1996).

58 *Barrow bought an interest:* Dennis DeValeria and Jeanne Burke DeValeria, *Honus Wagner: A Biography* (New York: Henry Holt, 1996).

58 *Persistent financial problems convinced:* Dennis DeValeria and Jeanne Burke DeValeria, *Honus Wagner: A Biography* (New York: Henry Holt, 1996).

60 *The following season was a disappointing one:* Dennis DeValeria and Jeanne Burke DeValeria, *Honus Wagner: A Biography* (New York: Henry Holt, 1996).

61 *Wagner's legacy, however, went beyond:* Dennis DeValeria and Jeanne Burke DeValeria, *Honus Wagner: A Biography* (New York: Henry Holt, 1996). Also see "Honus Wagner," Jan Finkel, Bioproj.SABR.org, and William Hageman, *Honus: The Life and Times of a Baseball Hero* (Champaign, Ill.: Sagamore, 1996).

CHAPTER 6: CITIZEN WAGNER

63 *Honus Wagner, abiding bachelor:* Dennis DeValeria and Jeanne Burke DeValeria, *Honus Wagner: A Biography* (New York: Henry Holt, 1996).

64 *He had already planted the seeds:* Dennis DeValeria and Jeanne Burke DeValeria, *Honus Wagner: A Biography* (New York: Henry Holt, 1996).

66 *Carnegie, Pennsylvania, was a vibrant immigrant community:* V. Robert Agostino, *A Track Through Time: A Centennial History of Carnegie, Pennsylvania* (Pittsburgh: Wolfson, 1994).

67 *In September 2004, Hurricane Ivan's heavy rains:* "Fire Guts Business District Recovering from Last Year's Flood," Associated Press, October 17, 2005. Also see "Borough Tallies Its Losses as Town Takes Stock of Damage," Carole Gilbert Brown, *Pittsburgh Post-Gazette*, September 22, 2004.

67 *Granddaughter Blair sold her Wagner memorabilia:* "Honus Wagner Memorabilia Brings More Than $271,000 in Online Auction," Joe Mandak, Associated Press, August 16, 2003. Also see "Honus' Treasures," Shelly Anderson, *Pittsburgh Post-Gazette*, June 13, 2003; and "Wagner's Granddaughter Treasures Her Memories," Shelly Anderson, *Pittsburgh Post-Gazette*, April 29, 2005.

68 *After years of neglect, Carnegie's political and business leaders:* "Residents to Vote on Site of Memorial to Wagner," Carole Gilbert Brown, *Pittsburgh Post-Gazette*, June 17, 1998; and "Town to Place Plaque for Honus Wagner," Carole Gilbert Brown, *Pittsburgh Post-Gazette*, June 24, 1998.

69 *The historical society was out of commission indefinitely:* "Honus Wagner's House Goes Up for Sale on eBay," David Guo, *Pittsburgh Post-Gazette*, June 22, 2006. Also see "Remembering Honus," David Guo, *Pittsburgh Post-Gazette*, June 22, 2005; "You and Honus Wagner Slept Here," Brian C. Rittmeyer, *Pittsburgh Tribune Review*, February 15, 2006; "Wagner B&B Plan Rejected," Brian C. Rittmeyer, *Pittsburgh Tribune Review*, February 16, 2006; "Businessman Pitches New Wagner Plan," Brian C. Rittmeyer, *Pittsburgh Tribune Review*, March 8, 2006; "Proposed Inn Fails to

Reach First Base," Bruce C. Rittmeyer, *Pittsburgh Tribune Review*, March 30, 2006; "Firm Hopes Honus Wagner's House Will Bring It Home," Brian C. Rittmeyer, *Pittsburgh Tribune Review*, June 9, 2006; "Honus Wagner's Spirit Lingers in Carnegie," Brian C. Rittmeyer, *Pittsburgh Tribune Review*, July 1, 2006.

70 *In a nation where deep-pocketed collectors:* "The Pitts: As All-Stars Come to Town, Pirates Ship Is Sinking," Michael O'Keeffe, *Daily News* (New York), July 9, 2006.

CHAPTER 7: HONUS GETS A MAKEOVER

72 *"For me it was an investment":* "Wagner's Wild Card: Mystery Has Surrounded Honus T206 Since 1909," Michael O'Keeffe and Bill Madden, *Daily News* (New York), March 25, 2001.

73 *McNall would plead guilty:* Pete Williams, *Card Sharks: How Upper Deck Turned a Child's Hobby into a High-Stakes, Billion-Dollar Business* (New York: Macmillan, 1995). Also see "McNall on Verge of an Early Release," Helene Elliott, *Los Angeles Times*, December 14, 2000.

73 *"Those legends just get greater and greater":* "Heads I Win, Tails You Lose," Christie Brown and Lisa Gubernick, *Forbes*, August 5, 1991.

73 *He bragged that he'd raked in $1,000:* "McNall's Fall: The Charade's Over," Roy MacGregor, *Ottawa Citizen*, November 29, 1994.

73 *It's easy to see how McNall:* "McNall's Fall: The Charade's Over," Roy MacGregor, *Ottawa Citizen*, November 29, 1994.

74 *McNall grew up in Arcadia, California:* "The Rise and McFall," Michael J. Goodman, *Sporting News*, March 18, 1996.

74 *"He always went for the high-priced stuff"*: "McNall's Fall: The Charade's Over," Roy MacGregor, *Ottawa Citizen*, November 29, 1994.

75 *McNall used his wealth*: "The Rise and (Big) Fall of Bruce Mc-Nall," Maureen Delany, *Press-Enterprise*, December 15, 1996.

75 *McNall was just as eager*: "McNall's Fall: The Charade's Over," Roy MacGregor, *Ottawa Citizen*, November 29, 1994.

75 *McNall understood that the Kings*: "McNall Details a Life of Temptations," Ray Turchansky, *Edmonton Journal*, August 3, 2003.

75 *McNall also formed a partnership*: Pete Williams, *Card Sharks: How Upper Deck Turned a Child's Hobby into a High-Stakes, Billion-Dollar Business* (New York: Macmillan, 1995).

76 *The price tag wasn't the only reason*: "$451,000 Wagner Card May Not Be in Mint Shape," John Leptich, *Chicago Tribune*, July 9, 1991.

76 *Alan Ray was a hockey fan*: "Wagner's Wild Card: Mystery Has Surrounded Honus T206 Since 1909," Michael O'Keeffe and Bill Madden, *Daily News* (New York), March 25, 2001.

CHAPTER 8: THE CARD GETS A PEDIGREE

89 *But before the mid-1970s*: Stephen Wong, *Smithsonian Baseball: Inside the World's Finest Private Collections* (New York: HarperCollins, 2005); Pete Williams, *Card Sharks: How Upper Deck Turned a Child's Hobby into a High-Stakes, Billion-Dollar Business* (New York: Macmillan, 1995); and "My Mentor Frank Nagy," Bill Mastro, MastroNet.com, December 2005.

90 *Bill Mastro's early years in the hobby*: Stephen Wong, *Smithsonian Baseball: Inside the World's Finest Private Collections* (New York: HarperCollins, 2005).

91 *Mastro befriended men like Frank Nagy:* "My Mentor Frank Nagy," Bill Mastro, Mastronet.com, December 2005.

92 *Mastro was at the hobby's first organized convention:* "Bill Mastro— The Ringmaster of Memorabilia," David Laurell, *Sports Market Report*, October 2005.

CHAPTER 9: MARVIN MONEY

96 *Thanks to Sy Berger:* Pete Williams, *Card Sharks: How Upper Deck Turned a Child's Hobby into a High-Stakes, Billion-Dollar Business* (New York: Macmillan, 1995).

96 *He became a ubiquitous presence . . . put it into motion:* Pete Williams, *Card Sharks: How Upper Deck Turned a Child's Hobby into a High-Stakes, Billion-Dollar Business* (New York: Macmillan, 1995).

98 *the player wouldn't get the $75 renewal fee:* Pete Williams, *Card Sharks: How Upper Deck Turned a Child's Hobby into a High-Stakes, Billion-Dollar Business* (New York: Macmillan, 1995).

99 *By 1972, Miller had amassed a war chest:* Pete Williams, *Card Sharks: How Upper Deck Turned a Child's Hobby into a High-Stakes, Billion-Dollar Business* (New York: Macmillan, 1995).

100 *The value of the card industry to baseball players:* Pete Williams, *Card Sharks: How Upper Deck Turned a Child's Hobby into a High-Stakes, Billion-Dollar Business* (New York: Macmillan, 1995).

101 Fleer Corp. v. Topps Chewing Gum, Inc., *opened the door:* Pete Williams, *Card Sharks: How Upper Deck Turned a Child's Hobby into a High-Stakes, Billion-Dollar Business* (New York: Macmillan, 1995).

102 *The rookie companies had just a few months:* Pete Williams, *Card Sharks: How Upper Deck Turned a Child's Hobby into a High-Stakes, Billion-Dollar Business* (New York: Macmillan, 1995).

103 *The Mantle card sold for about $700 in 1980:* Pete Williams, *Card Sharks: How Upper Deck Turned a Child's Hobby into a High-Stakes, Billion-Dollar Business* (New York: Macmillan, 1995).

CHAPTER 10: PSA AND THE DOCTORS

107 *PSA is a division of a publicly held company:* Annual Report, Collectors Universe, September 2005. Also see "Collectors Switch to Slab to Improve Cards' Value," Reid Creager, *Detroit Free Press*, March 3, 1999; and "Making the Grades," Diana Bosetti, *Orange County Business Journal*, February 3, 1997.

109 *The Wagner card generated headlines and gossip:* "On the Road; Grading Baseball Cards," *Inc.*, April 1, 1999.

112 *A few weeks after the card was graded:* "$451,000 Wagner Card May Not Be in Mint Shape," John Leptich, *Chicago Tribune*, July 9, 1991.

CHAPTER 11: FALL OF A KING

113 *"A ten-year period with discovery":* "The Rise and McFall," Michael J. Goodman, *Sporting News*, March 18, 1996.

114 *But GQ magazine estimated:* "The Rise and McFall," Michael J. Goodman, *Sporting News*, March 18, 1996. Also see "Heads I Win, Tails You Lose," Christie Brown and Lisa Gubernick, *Forbes*, August 5, 1991; "Spectacular Fall of a Big-Shot," Phil Reeves, *Independent*, February 28, 1995; "The Fall of a King," D'Arcy Jenish, *Macleans*, November 28, 1994; "The Rise and (Big) Fall of Bruce McNall," Maureen Delany, *Press-Enterprise*, December 15, 1996; "Four Years of Club Fed Anything but Relaxing for Mc-Nall," Greg Garber, ESPN.com, March 8, 2001; Pete Williams, *Card Sharks: How Upper Deck Turned a Child's Hobby into a High-Stakes, Billion-Dollar Business* (New York: Macmillan, 1995).

114 *He sold the team's Boeing 727:* "McNall's Fall: The Charade's Over," Rory MacGregor, *Ottawa Citizen*, November 29, 1994.

114 *The Kings even had to turn off the heat:* "The Rise and McFall," by Michael J. Goodman, *Sporting News*, March 18, 1996.

114 *Federal prosecutors charged McNall in November 1994:* "McNall Agrees to Plead to Fraud Charges," James Bates and Lisa Dillman, *Los Angeles Times*, November 15, 1994.

114 *Prosecutors said McNall obtained massive loans:* "The Rise and McFall," Michael J. Goodman, *Sporting News*, March 18, 1996; "The Rise and (Big) Fall of Bruce McNall," Maureen Delany, *Press-Enterprise*, December 15, 1996.

115 *Employees of McNall Sports and Entertainment:* "McNall Agrees to Plead to Fraud Charges," James Bates and Lisa Dillman, *Los Angeles Times*, November 15, 1994.

115 *McNall even stung his pal Gretzky:* "McNall Agrees to Plead to Fraud Charges," James Bates and Lisa Dillman, *Los Angeles Times*, November 15, 1994.

115 *The Great One visited him in jail:* "Honoring the Great One," Rich Hammond, *Daily News of Los Angeles*, October 10, 2002.

115 *Gretzky bid $225,000 for McNall's share:* "Gretzky Agrees to Card Deal," James Bates, *Los Angeles Times*, February 17, 1995.

116 *Treat Entertainment was about to put:* "Card Sharps," Rod Taylor, *Promo*, July 1, 2005; "Honus Wagner Card Offered in Give-away," Jay D. Preble, *Tampa Tribune*, October 10, 1995; "As a Treat, Company Will Give Away Wagner Card," Ruth Sadler, *Baltimore Sun*, February 24, 1996.

117 *By the time Treat Entertainment:* "Spinning Their Wheels: Baseball Card Market Has Gone Flat Since Glory Days of 1991,"

Greg Johnson, *Los Angeles Times*, July 29, 2006; "How Baseball Cards Lost Their Luster," Dave Jamieson, Salon.com, July 25, 2006; "House of Cards," John Garrity, *Sports Illustrated*, July 29, 1996; "Players Union Lures Kids Back to Baseball Cards," Julia Angwin, *Wall Street Journal*, May 11, 2006.

120 *To drum up publicity for the giveaway:* "As a Treat, Company Will Give Away Wagner Card," Ruth Sadler, *Baltimore Sun*, February 24, 1996; "Wagner Card Displayed, Presented," Bob Diamond, *Miami Herald*, March 8, 1996; "$450,000 Wagner Card on Display Today at Wal-Mart," Jerry Greene, *Orlando Sentinel*, January 10, 1996.

120 *The drawing for the grand prize was held on February 24, 1996:* *Larry King Weekend* transcript, CNN, February 24, 1996.

122 *"I feel like I won the lottery":* "Batting a Thousand: Baseball Gained a Fan When She Hit One Out of the Ballpark," Bob French, *South Florida Sun-Sentinel*, March 12, 1996.

122 *Gibbs was deluged with calls:* "Secret Life of the Record Honus Wagner Card," Dorothy S. Gelatt, *Maine Antique Digest*, December 1996.

122 *The promotion was a big success:* "Card Sharks," Rod Taylor, *Promo*, July 1, 2005.

124 *By 2005, annual sales of new trading cards:* "Spinning Their Wheels: Baseball Card Market Has Gone Flat Since Glory Days of 1991," Greg Johnson, *Los Angeles Times*, July 29, 2006; "How Baseball Cards Lost Their Luster," Dave Jamieson, Salon.com, July 25, 2006.

125 *In July 2006, as Topps' promotions staff:* "Bottom of the Ninth for Topps," Michael J. de la Merced, *New York Times*, July 28, 2006.

125 *Donruss, meanwhile, had been pushed:* "Players Union Lures Kids Back to Baseball Cards," Julia Angwin, *Wall Street Journal*, May 11, 2006.

CHAPTER 12: THE COLLECTOR

132 *The* Chicago Sun-Times *once described:* "Chicago's Card Shark," Bob Kurson, *Chicago Sun-Times*, January 26, 1997. Also see "What, Me Collect," Elliott Harris, *Chicago Sun-Times*, January 13, 2000; "His MAD Desire Makes Perfect Sense," Danielle Arnet, *Chicago Sun-Times*, March 22, 2000.

138 *Once it became clear to Gidwitz:* "Honus Wagner Card Could Fetch $1 Million," Marv Schneider, Associated Press, June 6, 2000; "Wagner Card Set for a $1M At-Bat," Owen Moritz, *Daily News* (New York), June 7, 2000; "Wagner's Wild Card: Mystery Has Surrounded Honus T206 Since 1909," Michael O'Keeffe and Bill Madden, *Daily News* (New York), March 25, 2001; "Collector Michael Gidwitz to Auction Off Honus Wagner Baseball Card," *CBS News* transcript, CBS, July 5, 2000.

CHAPTER 13: AIN'T NOTHIN' LIKE THE REAL THING

141 *"He's still mad at me":* "It's Not About My Legacy," Ann McDaniel and Jon Meacham, *Newsweek*, August 7, 2000.

144 *"I fully recognize that there are those who think":* Edward Wharton Tigar with AJ Wilson, *Burning Bright: The Autobiography of Edward Wharton Tigar* (London: Metal Bulletin Books, 1987).

CHAPTER 14: LOST AND FOUND

147 *In 2001 a Philadelphia family found a box:* "MastroNet Officials Elated About Find of T206 Wagner with Piedmont Back," T. S. O'Connell, *Sports Collectors Digest*, October 19, 2001.

148 *In 2002, meanwhile, a man who had just recently moved:* "Florida Man Makes Huge T206 Attic Find," T. S. O'Connell, *Sports Collectors Digest*, April 20, 2002.

149 *Even bureaucrats have caught T206 gold fever:* "Treasurer's Office Finds Potentially Valuable 91-Year-Old Baseball Card," Associated Press, August 16, 2000. Also see "Unearthed Baseball Card Could be Worth $1 Million," Rick Steelhammer, *Charleston Gazette*, August 16, 2000.

149 *But unfortunately for West Virginia:* "State Officials Thrown a Curve; Wagner Card Is a Reproduction," Rick Steelhammer, *Charleston Gazette*, August 25, 2000. Also see "Not in the Cards," Anya Sostek, *Governing*, November 2000.

151 *For more than a decade, John Cobb and Ray Edwards:* "The Holy Grail: $1M Card Hits eBay, But Is It Real?" Michael O'Keeffe, *Daily News* (New York), November 20, 2005. Also see "How to Put a Price on a Dream?" Paul Daugherty, *Cincinnati Enquirer*, May 23, 2004; "Big Payday May Not Be in Cards," Michael Hirsley, *Chicago Tribune*, August 16, 2006.

CHAPTER 15: FAKES AND FRAUDS

163 *On a summer day in 1972, a thief slipped:* "Cooperstown Hall of Fame," Michael O'Keeffe and Bill Madden, *Daily News* (New York), August 20, 2000.

166 *The Hall of Fame would find itself:* "Storied Mitt Caught in Hall Controversy," Michael O'Keeffe, *Daily News* (New York), November 25, 2001.

169 *North Carolina collector Ralph Perullo:* "What Wood Joltin' Joe Say About This?" Michael O'Keeffe, *Daily News* (New York), June 6, 2004.

170 *The role Bushing and Knoll played*: "Slugging It Out," Michael O'Keeffe, *Daily News* (New York), January 16, 2005.

174 *The DiMaggio glove is not*: "Bidder Beware," Michael O'Keeffe and Bill Madden, *Daily News* (New York), May 14, 2000.

CHAPTER 16: A WHITE KNIGHT

178 *"Dear Robert Edward Auctions"*: "Letter from Michael Gidwitz," RobertEdwardAuctions.com, September 1, 2004.

180 *Under the heading,* "No Conflicts of Interest": "Absolutely No Conflicts of Interest," RobertEdwardAuctions.com.

181 *Noe was the Bush-Cheney campaign chairman*: "It's a Flip of 'Coin' Probe," Michael O'Keeffe, *Daily News* (New York), June 18, 2006.

184 *Which is exactly what happened to Tony Cocchi*: "More Fraud on the Market," Michael O'Keeffe, *Daily News* (New York), May 21, 2006.

CHAPTER 17: MILLION-DOLLAR BABY

187 *At an age when most young men*: "For Some, an Outdated Ad; For Others, the Mona Lisa," Bill Shaikin, *Los Angeles Times*, July 19, 2000.

187 *Seigel was born in Toronto*: "Holding the Trump Card," Andre Mouchard, *Orange County Register*, July 27, 2000; and Stephen Wong, *Smithsonian Baseball: Inside the World's Finest Private Collections* (New York: HarperCollins, 2005).

189 *"I still can't believe we did it"*: "OC Man Pays Major League Price for Card," Bill Shaikin, *Los Angeles Times*, July 19, 2000.

189 *"If Dad can spend $1 million on a baseball card"*: "For Some, an Outdated Ad; For Others, the Mona Lisa," Bill Shaikin, *Los Angeles Times*, July 19, 2000.

192 *It was displayed at the Ronald Reagan:* "Memorabilia on Display at Reagan Library," Rich Romine, *Ventura County Star,* March 2, 2003.

192 *"If I had a million dollars":* "Westpack Students Treated to Look at $1.3-Million Honus Wagner Card," Joan Hansen, *Orange County Register,* November 1, 2001.

196 *Rumors began swirling in September 2006:* "Haggle Over Honus Card Begins Again," Michael O'Keeffe, *Daily News* (New York), October 1, 2006.

AUTHORS' NOTE

Most of the information presented in this book comes from interviews conducted over the course of several years. We spoke to dozens of sources from the world of trading cards and sports memorabilia, including collectors, dealers, auction-house executives, grading-service officials, and memorabilia authenticators. In addition, we conducted extensive interviews with law-enforcement officials and representatives of Major League Baseball, the Major League Baseball Players Association, and the National Baseball Hall of Fame. Most of our sources were interviewed numerous times.

Some of the collectors and collectibles-industry officials who provided information for this book agreed to talk only after we guaranteed them anonymity. We tried to avoid using information from anonymous sources whenever possible, and when we did use such information, we verified it with at least one other source.

In addition to our interviews, we relied on numerous books, newspaper stories, magazine articles, and Web sites. One of the most important sources is *Card Sharks* by Pete Williams (Macmillan, 1995), which provides not just an exhaustive history of the Upper Deck company but also a fascinating look at the history of baseball cards and collecting.

Collectors who wish to learn more about the T206 series should see Scot A. Reader's *Inside T206: A Collector's Guide to the Classic Baseball Card Set*. Reader is a first-class researcher with a breezy writing style. T206Museum.com is a terrific Web site both for novice and veteran collectors. David Rudd Cycleback's "A Brief History of Baseball Cards," posted on Cycleback.com, is a terrific primer for the early days of trading cards and collector.

Honus Wagner: A Biography by Dennis DeValeria and Jeanne Burke DeValeria (Henry Holt, 1996) is a tremendous resource for baseball fans who hope to learn more about Wagner, among the greatest players in baseball history. Another great resource on Wagner was written by Jan Finkel of the Society for American Baseball Research; it can be found on the Web at Bioproj.SABR.org.

Marcella McGrogan and Carol Dlugos at the Historical Society of Carnegie were great sources of information about Honus Wagner and his hometown, and we thank them for their time, patience, and unabashed love of baseball's roots. Sports collectibles veteran Shelly Jaffe was an invaluable font of knowledge about the history of the hobby. Robert Plancich was also a vital source, overloading our e-mail inboxes with updates from his crusade to clean up the sports collectibles industry. We are also grateful to Dennis Esken, who knows more about baseball and baseball gloves than anybody, and Bill Heitman, a monster of card collecting. Our appreciation goes to Marvin Miller, a marvelous storyteller and one of the most influential men in baseball history—his card should be worth a million dollars.

Our gratitude to Jake Elwell for seeing the potential, and Mauro DiPreta for seeing the project through.

We thank our colleagues at the New York *Daily News*. They produce the best damn sports section in America every day. Special thanks go to Bill Madden, who shared his encyclopedic knowledge of baseball, cards, and collectibles whenever we had a question. We'd also like to thank T. J. Quinn, Christian Red, Leon Carter, Jim Rich, Bill Gallo, Mike Lupica, Ed Fay, and Wayne Coffey for their friendship and support and Martin Dunn for giving us the green light. Sally Otos and Cheryl Thompson were invaluable resources. The Harrises—Paul, Sitta, Caroline and Charlotte—were an inspiration. They showed us what real fans are all about.

Thanks again to Nancy Thompson for her wit, skill, and patience.

And an extra-special thanks to Rob Lifson, who was unfailingly generous with his time, knowledge, and expertise, and Mike Gidwitz, who took us on a fascinating trip into the mind of a first-rate collector. Guys, we now know the difference between a Gold Border and a White Border.